9-91

DATE DUE

DEMCO 38-296

GREAT WRITERS OF THE ENGLISH LANGUAGE

Early English Writers

STAFF CREDITS

Executive Editor
Reg Wright

Series Editor
Sue Lyon

Editors
Jude Welton
Sylvia Goulding

Deputy Editors
Alice Peebles
Theresa Donaghey

Features Editors
Geraldine McCaughrean
Emma Foa
Ian Chilvers

Art Editors
Kate Sprawson
Jonathan Alden
Helen James

Designers
Simon Wilder
Frank Landamore

Senior Picture Researchers
Julia Hanson
Vanessa Fletcher
Georgina Barker

Picture Clerk
Vanessa Cawley

Production Controllers
Judy Binning
Tom Helsby

Editorial Secretaries
Fiona Bowser
Sylvia Osborne

Managing Editor
Alan Ross

Editorial Consultant
Maggi McCormick

Publishing Manager
Robert Paulley

Reference Edition Published 1989
Published by Marshall Cavendish Corporation
147 West Merrick Road
Freeport, Long Island
N.Y. 11520

Typeset by Litho Link Ltd., Welshpool
Printed and Bound in Italy by
L.E.G.O. S.p.a. Vicenza

LIBRARY OF CONGRESS
Library of Congress Cataloging-in-Publication Data
Great Writers of the English Language
   p. cm.
   Includes index vol.
   ISBN 1-85435-000-5 (set): $399.95
   1. English literature — History and criticism. 2. English
literature — Stories, plots, etc. 3. American literature — History
and criticism. 4. American literature — Stories, plots, etc.
5. Authors. English — Biography. 6. Authors. American — Biography.
I. Marshall Cavendish Corporation.
PR85.G66 1989
820'.9 – dc19   88-21077
                                                        CIP

ISBN 1–85435–000–5 (set)
ISBN 1–85435–001–3 (vol)

GREAT WRITERS OF THE ENGLISH LANGUAGE

Early English Writers

William Shakespeare

Samuel Pepys

John Bunyan

Henry Fielding

MARSHALL CAVENDISH · NEW YORK · TORONTO · LONDON · SYDNEY

PREFACE

BY ANTHONY BURGESS

Those of us who have spent much of a long lifetime reading and re-reading occasionally play the game of assembling imaginary first elevens, usually with a twelfth man (or, of course, woman). Who are the dozen greatest of the great authors? Or – and this is much more difficult – which are the twelve books that stand head and shoulders above all the others? I have played the author game often, and on each occasion the team has been different, except for Shakespeare, who is inevitably the captain. As for the twelve desert island books, the question of choice is so often a question of mood, of temporary enchantment or, looking at it negatively, of temporary revulsion. The list of great authors and their works which, I take it, was the original skeleton of this series is not likely to please everybody all the time, but, so capricious are we in our wretched humanity, there will always be a mood when we can accept *Love for Lydia* as a representative modern novel and not be too unhappy that Shakespeare's history plays have been ignored. After all, we can all grow bored with Falstaff or sick of being exhorted to hate the French in *Henry V*.

Get the major critics of our age together to decide on the great modern novels, and they would all, without exception, rate Joyce's *Ulysses* high above Galsworthy's *Forsyte Saga*. But there is a sense in which literary greatness does not cohere with sheer reading enjoyment. If I say that I enjoy re-reading *Ulysses* and have never got any real kick out of the *Forsyte Saga,* then I will rightly be regarded as an eccentric. If I say, which I frequently do, that the greatest British novel of the twentieth century is Ford Madox Ford's *Parade's End*, then a verdict of unsound mind is likely to be laid on me. And if, which I do as little as possible, I extol Milton's *Paradise Lost* as the supreme poetic achievement of the language, then a charge of hypocrisy would be in order. For I do not like *Paradise Lost.*

The point about all the books considered in this series is that they are enjoyable. When I was young and bumptious I used to talk about our all having a duty to literature, meaning an obligation to read the tedious but uplifting (like *The Wealth of Nations* and the whole of *The Decline and Fall of the Roman Empire*). I learned a great lesson from my old friend Vladimir Nabokov, the author of *Lolita*, who used to say that a book was either for the bedside or the wastepaper basket. If we are totally honest about literature, we will be forced to admit that a great deal of what is admired, though not necessarily read, is for the wastepaper basket. The essays of Charles Lamb, for instance, or Spenser's *Fairy Queen*. Those are for my wastepaper basket: you may stuff into yours what you please, so long as you have tried to read it first. The point about all the books dealt with in this series is that they are for the bedside. Ideally they require a long convalescence with plenty of grapes and cool drinks.

More than anything, this series is dedicated to the joy of reading, than which no living joy is greater. Drink fuddles, food surfeits, sex is playing into the hands of biology. But reading never palls. A book is a miracle. Its format was so perfect when it was first invented that modern technology has never been able to improve on it. It does not have to be plugged into the wall or fed with batteries. Where television provides a mere innutritious snack for the eye, a good book nourishes the entire human system through the channel of the imagination. All the books that are considered here are good books. To declare them all great would be to go too far, and there will be readers who will shake their heads gravely at the imputation of greatness to writers like John Steinbeck or Mrs Gaskell. But greatness has never properly been defined. Whoever gives great pleasure is probably great enough.

© Anthony Burgess June 1988

Anthony Burgess is an English novelist and critic of international renown. The author of many novels including Clockwork Orange *(1962) and* Earthly Powers *(1980) he has also written books on Hemmingway, Joyce and Shakespeare. His autobiography* Little Wilson and Big God *was published in 1987 and he is a contributor to* The Times Literary Supplement, Hudson Review, American Scholar *and* Le Monde *among other periodicals.*

CONTENTS

INTRODUCTION 6

INTRODUCTION

No one has succeeded in explaining why some men and women break out of the ranks of the talented and go on to become great writers. Mysteriously, one maiden lady among the many thousands in Regency England has a gift for satire and an insight into character that enable her to write *Pride and Prejudice*; just as, a century later, one young Mid-westerner captures the hectic, delusive glamour of the 1920s with a poetic intensity that makes *The Great Gatsby* a modern classic. Such outstanding works are not simply the best satires and romantic elegies of their period in history: they are unageing monuments of genius that transcend and defy classification.

LIVING TRADITIONS

But although there is no accounting for individual talent, it is clear that great writers as a species do not spring up from barren ground, but are nourished by strong, living traditions. In this respect the English-speaking peoples have been particularly fortunate. For hundreds of years, their history, language and literature have been extraordinarily rich, reverberating with conflict and diversity, and yet effectively unbroken in continuity. And in that time 'English literature', confined to two of Europe's ·offshore islands, has given way to 'literature in English' as the United States and many former possessions of the British Empire have developed their own distinctive cultures and ways of using the language.

To help overcome obstacles created by the passage of time GREAT WRITERS OF THE ENGLISH LANGUAGE has been created. The world mirrored by literature has changed radically, and society, technology, morals, manners and ideals have all been affected. So have the political, social and religious situations that condition or energize the creative imagination: we are no longer familiar with the world of Chaucer's pilgrims, Rudyard Kipling's heroic colonial administrators, or even John Steinbeck's dispossessed migrant workers, even if we can respond to the authors' splendid language and narrative skills. Moreover literary styles, techniques and forms have been influenced by changes in sensibility, literary fashion, and the nature of the audience the writer hopes to reach. Chaucer, composing narrative poems to be read aloud at court, was patently engaged in a different

sort of enterprise from the poet-playwright William Shakespeare writing for 16th century Londoners; and neither worked in the same vein as the modern novelist who hopes to reach a mass international audience via paperbacks.

This means that any great literary work of the past, however gripping, will become much more enriching if the reader knows at least something of the author's life, works and inspiration. Each chapter of GREAT WRITERS OF THE ENGLISH LANGUAGE is therefore divided into a number of sections, arranged for maximum interest and usefulness.

'The Writer's Life' presents the biographical facts, revealing the men and women whose experiences and personalities lie behind the masterpieces.

The 'Reader's Guide' explores one of the writer's classic works, summarizing its plot (without giving too much away!), describing all the important characters, and attempting to identify the elements that constitute its greatness; in combination with 'Works in Outline', a brief conducted tour round the author's other significant writings, it provides a useful overall view of a lifetime's creative achievement. By contrast, 'Writer at Work' takes us into the author's study to examine the literary process itself – the techniques and themes involved.

Great literature does not necessarily mirror the real world in a straightforward fashion, but it undoubtedly draws on it, 'Sources and Inspiration' describes some crucial aspect of the world in which the writer lived – one so deeply experienced that it gave rise to powerful and compelling narratives and images.

Works of literature need to be located in relation to one another and to the historical circumstances in which they were conceived and written. The remainder of this introduction is therefore devoted to a brief, more or less chronological outline of literature in English, describing changes in tastes, styles and forms in the context of historical change.

Written literature in English began in the 6th century A.D. with Anglo-Saxon, and persisted even after the Norman Conquest of 1066 made French dominant for a time. But this 'Old English' can now only be read in the original by specialists; for most of us 'English literature' begins in the late 14th century, when English and French had fused into 'Middle English'

and produced the greatest poet of the English Middle Ages, Geoffrey Chaucer.

Chaucer's *Canterbury Tales* is a long narrative poem in which a group of pilgrims agrees that each of them shall tell a story to help pass the time on the journey. This type of narrative framework was already popular in continental Europe, and was only one of many debts that Chaucer owed to the new literary movements originating in Italy. As the creator of a group of stories ranging from the fantastic to the bawdy, and a series of vigorous, slyly observed character studies, Chaucer has often been called the first English novelist.

INTRODUCTION OF PRINTING

The introduction of printing by William Caxton in the 15th century revolutionized communications and strengthened the emergent sense of national identity in England and elsewhere, leading to the development of an authoritative, standardized 'book' language. In choosing the speech of London and the court for his printed works, Caxton largely determined the future of literary English.

The 16th century has often been described as the beginning of the modern era. Tudor monarchs such as Henry VIII (1509-47) and Elizabeth I (1558-1603) created a strong national state, and the impact of two European phenomena, the Renaissance and the Reformation, transformed the English mind and English culture. The Renaissance imposed on English education and literature a 'classical' stamp that was to survive for centuries. But although Latin retained its prestige as a medium for 'serious' writing, other forces favoured increasing use of the vernacular (that is, the native language, in this instance English) in both poetry and prose.

One of these forces was the Protestant Reformation begun by Martin Luther. Use of the vernacular in services and access for all to the Scriptures were key Protestant teachings, and even before the final triumph of Protestantism under Queen Elizabeth, the Bible had been translated into English and the almost equally influential *Book of Common Prayer* had been issued by Archbishop Cranmer. Early in the following century the King James Bible, or Authorized Version, appeared; its phrases and cadences were to permeate the thoughts and words of many generations of men and women throughout the English-speaking world.

The Renaissance influence was strongest in poetry. In Henry VIII's reign Sir Thomas Wyatt introduced the sonnet from the Continent, and the Earl of Surrey wrote the earliest poetry in blank verse – the highly adaptable unrhymed verse-form that was to become the main vehicle for works of high ambition, employed by Shakespeare, Milton, Wordsworth and many others. The last 20 years of Queen Elizabeth's reign were a golden age, crowded with outstanding poets such as Edmund Spenser and Sir Philip Sidney, who also wrote the first significant work of literary criticism in English, *An Apology for Poetry*.

BIRTH OF THE THEATRE

The same period witnessed the birth of the modern drama, and in 1576 the first public playhouse was opened in London. It was soon followed by rival establishments, and the demand for plays attracted impecunious university men desperate enough to attempt to live by the pen. They brought the Renaissance versions of classical tragedy and comedy to the English stage, and the greatest of the 'university wits', Christopher Marlowe, wrought the blank-verse tragedy into a formidable instrument, ready for an even greater writer – William Shakespeare.

Shakespeare's pre-eminence in English literature, both as poet and playwright, has seldom been disputed during the last 300 years. He was equally at home in tragedy, comedy and tragi-comedy. His long sequence of sonnets represents the highest excellence ever achieved in that difficult form, as well as offering tantalizing glimpses of a private emotional tangle whose precise significance eludes us. But his plays function on an even higher level, for in their best moments poetry, character and situation are fused in supreme literary expression.

The 17th century was a period of political and religious crises, during which England experienced a civil war and became a republic for a few years (1649-60). The zealous reforming spirit of puritanism dominated political and cultural life, and in 1642 the playhouses were closed, causing a significant break in English theatrical history.

In 1660 King Charles II was restored to the throne, and a strong reaction set in against puritanism, puritans in their turn suffering persecution. Among those imprisoned was a tinker-preacher named John Bunyan. He wrote one of the world's most famous books, *The Pilgrim's Progress* (1676), employing the almost defunct technique of allegory (in which the 'char-

acters' are abstract qualities) to fashion an archetypal story of the soul's 'pilgrimage'.

By about 1690 England's worst internal crises were past. The earlier 18th century became known as the Augustan Age, a label that implied the existence of an urbane, highly civilized and relatively secure society. Verse tended to be adroit and accomplished rather than passionate, although the outstanding poet, Alexander Pope, was a master of satire and invective. The greatest master of plain and vigorous prose during this period was Jonathan Swift, an Irishman, whose masterpiece is *Gulliver's Travels* (1726). Ironically, this savage indictment of humanity is constructed around a story that has delighted the world ever since, and has become most widely known of all in versions devised for children.

Like Bunyan and Swift, Daniel Defoe created a work whose imaginary central situation appealed to readers on some fundamental level, making it a universal favourite. This was the story of the solitary castaway *Robinson Crusoe* (1719). In this and other books Defoe in fact used real people and events as sources for narratives which he always cast in the first person, taking pains to make them seem like genuine autobiographies. Also important was Henry Fielding, who in *Tom Jones* (1749) used the novel to give a wide-ranging, good-humoured picture of English society.

THE ROMANTIC ERA

The emergence of the novel – from allegory and fable into a convincing narrative of social and psychological interest – was a major literary event. It was a reflection, and to a considerable extent a product, of the 18th century's increasing social fluidity and secular, urban and commercial outlook, which favoured the matter-of-factness that tended to be characteristic of the novel. But towards the end of the century a reaction set in against 'the Age of Reason' and the Romantic movement was born. Romanticism influenced the whole of Europe and took many related forms; in Britain it was above all a great poetic revolution. The pioneering works of the poet William Blake were followed by the *Lyrical Ballads* (1798) of William Wordsworth and Samuel Taylor Coleridge, whose famous preface rejected the dry reasonableness and decorous language of most 18th-century poetry.

Of the younger generation of poets, John Keats, Percy Bysshe Shelley and Lord Byron, Byron, though not necessarily the greatest of the Romantic poets, had the widest influence, making the dark, brood-

ing 'Byronic' hero a ubiquitous figure in Romantic literature.

Romanticism also influenced the novel. Pseudo-medieval mysteries, horrors and occult occurrences characterized the 'Gothic' novel, which creaks and clanks too loudly for 20th-century tastes; but the genre did produce one of the most potent of modern myths in *Frankenstein* (1818), written by 19-year-old Mary Shelley, the poet's wife. One of the book's admirers was Sir Walter Scott, whose Romanticism took a quite different form. Between 1814 and 1832 the incredibly industrious and prolific Scott created the historical novel in its now accepted form.

Although in Britain its most powerful surge was spent by 1825, Romanticism remained an important element in the 19th-century imagination. Occasionally it still erupted into full view, notably in *Wuthering Heights* (1847) and *Jane Eyre* (1847) by the sisters Emily and Charlotte Brontë. However, the main thrust of the novel was towards a faithful portrayal of men and women in their social relationships – a form of literature in which women writers, disadvantaged in many other spheres, also proved able to excel.

In *Pride and Prejudice* (1813) and other novels, Jane Austen directed her good-tempered irony at genteel provincial society in Regency England. The world she described was soon greatly altered by the accelerating Industrial Revolution, which turned Britain into 'the Workshop of the World' in the early years of Queen Victoria's reign (1837-1901). A galaxy of great Victorian novelists – Charles Dickens, William Makepeace Thackeray, George Eliot, Mrs Elizabeth Gaskell, Anthony Trollope – appeared in the middle years of the century and between them gave a near-comprehensive account of British society. Some, like George Eliot and Mrs Gaskell, looked back nostalgically on the old rural England that was rapidly passing away, although they also described the newly dominant middle class and the abominable conditions of industrial workers and the slum poor. His own early struggles and London in all its grandeur and squalor were the principal inspirations of Dickens, whose performances as universal entertainer and social reformer won him the title of 'the National Sparkler'. By contrast, his contemporary and rival Thackeray, at heart a more conservative writer, satirized the manners and morals of the immediate past in *Vanity Fair* (1848).

Meanwhile the United States was beginning to produce writers of international stature. Edgar Allen Poe wrote short stories such as *The Fall of the House of Usher* (1839) in his own distinctively macabre idiom, and also pioneered the detective story in *The Murders in the Rue Morgue* (1841). Nathaniel Hawthorne looked into the dark heart of the puritan tradition in *The Scarlet Letter* (1850), and in *Moby Dick* (1851) his friend Herman Melville transformed a whaling expedition into a terrifying, eccentric metaphysical adventure that found little response among readers until the 20th century. Curiously enough, such distinctively American subjects as the frontier, the pioneer spirit and the democratic outlook found no great writers to celebrate them until Walt Whitman wrote the poems collected as *Leaves of Grass* (1885) and Mark Twain published *Huckleberry Finn* (1884) and other novels which were thoroughly American in flavour if not always gentle in their handling of American failings.

Late 19th century literature was increasingly diverse, ranging from Kipling's exotic splendours of British India (*Kim*, 1901), Robert Louis Stevenson's colourful historical novels such as *Treasure Island* (1883), to the 'decadent' extreme of Oscar Wilde in the 1890s with *The Picture of Dorian Gray* (1891).

Also a product of the 1890s were the 'scientific romances' of H. G. Wells, the father-figure of all modern science fiction as well as a prolific novelist and influential social prophet. The detective story too became a popular genre in this period; building on the pioneering work of Edgar Allen Poe and Wilkie Collins, Sir Arthur Conan Doyle provided an ubiquitously influential pattern for tales of mystery, suspense and sleuthing in his Sherlock Holmes stories.

Novels on a more ambitious scale continued to be written, often with a more realistic view of sexual and social relationships than their mid-Victorian predecessors. However, the reading public was easily scandalized, and even Thomas Hardy, already a famous and respected writer, was so fiercely attacked after the appearance of *Tess of the D'Urbervilles* (1891) that he gave up writing novels. Only a few years later the publication of *The Way of All Flesh* (1903) after the death of its author, Samuel Butler, was immediately seen as the end of an epoch, since its hostile picture of Victorian life coincided with the beginning of the more permissive Edwardian era.

Nineteenth-century novels tended to be more notable for their vitality and abundance than for their formal artistic qualities. The American Henry James settled in England and demonstrated in his huge fictional output (including *The Portrait of a Lady*, 1881) that the novel could be a consciously wrought work of art, gaining immensely in subtlety through a skilful manipulation of narrative devices.

However, robust talents continued to emerge during the Edwardian period. This was the heyday of H. G. Wells, Arnold Bennett and John Galsworthy, author of *The Forsyte Saga* (1906-21). Though social criticism and socialist ideas were prominent in fiction and the drama, writers tended to be buoyed up by a feeling that life was improving and could be improved further.

THE TWENTIETH CENTURY

The mass slaughter of World War I (1914-18) destroyed Edwardian certainties. The most immediate response came from the 'War Poets', young men who fought (and in most cases died) in the conflict: the verses of Rupert Brooke, Wilfred Owen, Siegfried Sassoon, Isaac Rosenberg and others constitute a poet's progress through barrage and battle, from enthusiasm to outrage and grief.

By the 1920s there was a marked trend towards literary experimentalism, labelled 'modernism'. The abandonment of conventional forms, allusiveness, and concentration on the isolated individual rather than social relationships were characteristic of modernism; some or all of them are found in, for example, James Joyce's *Ulysses* (1922) and the poems of T. S. Eliot, Ezra Pound and the later W. B. Yeats. Equally striking was the new interest of writers in the fragmentary nature of consciousness and other non-rational forces, an interest certainly stimulated by Sigmund Freud's psychoanalytical discoveries. Unarticulated shifts in emotion haunt the stories of the New Zealander Katherine Mansfield, while Virginia Woolf, like Joyce, tried to capture the moment-by-moment quality of experience through the 'stream of consciousness' technique.

Deep unconscious forces sweep the characters along in the novels and stories of D. H. Lawrence; on occasion his sexual mysticism proved too much for contemporary watchdogs of morality, and the full text of his novel *Lady Chatterley's Lover* (1928) was not published until 1960.

In fact the traditional novel continued to flourish in the period between the wars, although authors were far more conscious of technique than their 19th-century predecessors. E. M. Forster's career as a writer of fiction ended abruptly with *A Passage to India* (1924), in its time an important anti-colonial statement; but his sensitive concern for personal relationships has made his work of continuing interest. William Somerset Maugham's *Of Human Bondage* (1915) is a classic autobiographical novel; Maugham's stoical realism, distinctive personal voice and gift for story-telling gained his books a world-wide following in the 1920s. Two younger writers, Aldous Huxley and Evelyn Waugh, held the glass of satire up to the vices and follies of their time; both were fundamentally serious, but whereas Waugh's Catholicism encouraged him to scourge contemporary morals, Huxley's intellectual humanism led him to probe the future in the hope of averting the doom or dehumanization most memorably evoked in *Brave New World* (1932).

AMERICAN NOVELISTS

In the first half of the 20th century the United States produced a literature second to none. Apart from the poets Eliot and Pound, and playwright Eugene O'Neill, there were many novelists of distinction. By contrast with the massive naturalism of Theodore Dreiser and the racy, documentary approach of Sinclair Lewis, F. Scott Fitzgerald was a graceful sophisticate with a singing style; an archetypal figure of the 1920s, in *The Great Gatsby* (1925) he gave the most poignant account of the conflict between the American Dream and American realities. Fitzgerald's friend Ernest Hemingway was more innovative and therefore more directly influential; he developed a spare, colloquial style that was widely copied. The Hemingway hero is essentially solitary, obsessed with testing his courage and risking his integrity in a violent world. However, even Hemingway responded to the changed mood of the 1930s, when the Great Depression and the rise of fascism suddenly made the 1920s seem frivolously hectic and irresponsible. In Hemingway's *For Whom the Bell Tolls* (1940), set during the Spanish Civil War, the hero embraces a cause and – despite its imperfections – is prepared to die for it. The same message of human solidarity is carried by John Steinbeck's *The Grapes of Wrath* (1939), the greatest novel produced by experience of the Depression.

In literature as in life, the 20th century has witnessed many new developments. Poetry, so popular among the Victorians, has been a minority taste since the advent of modernism. The novel, however, holds its place despite new media. No doubt, whatever forms they choose to employ in future, great writers will continue to produce works of genius in English for as long as the language lasts.

WILLIAM SHAKESPEARE

1564-1616

The greatest and most famous of English writers, Shakespeare
reigned supreme in the theatre at a particularly fertile period of
English drama. His career as actor/playwright took him from
Stratford to London, where he wrote his celebrated tragedies
in the first decade of the 16th century. Unmatched in his gift
for language, he created legendary characters and dramatic
moments which have inspired audiences and artists down to
the present day.

Immortal Bard

Shakespeare's dazzling theatrical career was based in London; but he regarded Stratford as his true home, his fellow playwright Ben Jonson dubbing him 'Sweet Swan of Avon'.

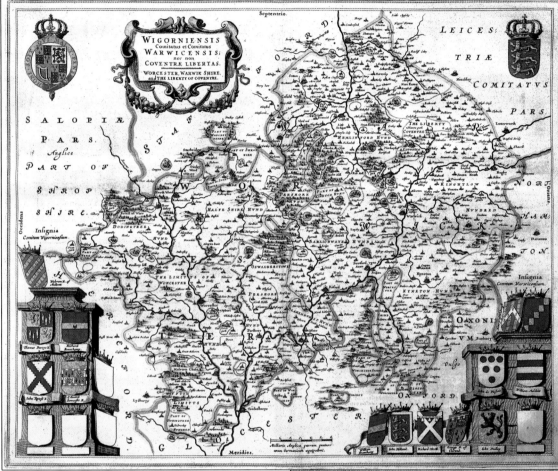

Heart of England
(left) The area of Warwickshire where Shakespeare grew up is noted for its beauty and historical richness – a fertile background for his work.

Family home
(below) Shakespeare is said to have been born in this house in Stratford's Henley Street. When his father died in 1601, Shakespeare inherited the property.

Unlike his plays, William Shakespeare's career was singularly undramatic, for he lived the life of a cautiously successful middle-class businessman. As far as we know, he never went abroad, and his life revolved around two towns: his native Stratford-upon-Avon in Warwickshire, with which he kept in touch all his life; and London, about 90 miles away, where he achieved a leading position as a man of the theatre – playwright, actor, and part-owner of the country's foremost theatrical company.

William Shakespeare was baptized in the parish church of Holy Trinity, Stratford, on 26 April 1564. We do not know exactly when he was born, but it is unlikely to have been more than a few days before this, and patriotic sentiment has settled on 23 April – St George's Day – as the most fitting date for the birth of England's greatest writer. He was the third child of John and Mary Shakespeare; two older sisters died in childhood, and later he had two more sisters and three brothers, about whom very little is known.

John Shakespeare was a glover, and he also traded in timber, wood and other commodities. The first record of him dates from 1552, when he was fined by the Stratford authorities for having an unlicensed dunghill or refuse heap in Henley Street, rather than using the 'comyn mukhyll'. This lapse was soon forgotten, however, and John prospered in his business and personal life. In 1556 he bought two houses in Henley Street and the following year he married Mary Arden, who was of a rather higher social class.

John Shakespeare came to own a considerable amount of property in Stratford and was one of the town's most respected citizens, holding a succession of public offices, including that of bailiff (mayor). Stratford at this time was, in the words of the contemporary antiquarian William Camden, a 'handsome small market town'. Its population was about 1500 when William Shakespeare was born, but in that very year the plague struck and 237 burials were recorded from July to December – roughly one in six of the inhabitants died.

Baby William was no doubt fortunate to survive his plague-ridden first year, but nothing is documented of this or the rest of his childhood. However, as the eldest son of one of the town's leading citizens, he would have received the best education available locally, and it is likely that he attended Stratford grammar school.

Shakespeare probably started at the school aged seven or eight, and would have been thoroughly steeped in Latin, doing little else for about eight hours a day, six days a week. It was probably during his schooldays that he first became stage-struck. Stratford had no theatre, but travelling players often performed there, and Shakespeare's father as bailiff had the duty of licensing them. It was no doubt in the Guildhall, immediately below his schoolroom, that young William saw his first plays.

Pupils usually attended the grammar school until they were about 15, but Shakespeare may have left earlier in order to help his father, who had run into financial difficulties. The next firm date we have in Shakespeare's life, however, is 1582, when, at the age of 18, he married Anne Hathaway, who was eight years his senior and

Schooldays
Shakespeare probably began his education at a petty (elementary) school, then spent about five or six years at Stratford grammar school (above), where he mastered Latin.

Anne Hathaway's Cottage
(left) Shakespeare's wife came from Shottery, just outside Stratford. Although known as Anne Hathaway's cottage, this house was her father's.

Royal patron
(above) Elizabeth I was an enthusiastic patron of the theatre. She had her own troupe of actors (the Queen's Men) and Shakespeare's company often performed for her.

three-months pregnant. She came from a land-owning family at a nearby village, but nothing is known about her personally.

The ceremony took place in November and a daughter, Susanna, was born in May 1583; two more children – the twins Hamnet and Judith – followed in 1585. Because the marriage was evidently made in haste and because Shakespeare spent much of his later life away from his family in London, it has been surmised that the union was an unhappy one. However, there is no real evidence for this and Shakespeare certainly regarded Stratford as his permanent home.

Between the birth of his twins in 1585 and the first mention of him as a playwright in London in

Key Dates

1564 born in Stratford

1582 marries Anne Hathaway

1583 birth of daughter Susanna

1585 birth of twins Hamnet and Judith

1592 first mentioned as dramatist in London

c.1595 *Romeo and Juliet*

1596 death of son Hamnet

1597 buys New Place, Stratford

c.1600 *Hamlet*

1601 death of father

c.1605 *King Lear*

1608 mother dies

c.1610 retires to Stratford

1616 dies in Stratford

1623 publication of First Folio – earliest collected edition of his work

1592 there is no documentary evidence as to what Shakespeare was doing, and consequently this period has been called 'the missing years'. Predictably, there has been no shortage of theories to fill the gap, and because Shakespeare's work covers such a vast range of human experiences, it has been suggested he was a soldier, a sailor, a lawyer, and many other things. The 17th-century antiquary John Aubrey, however, wrote on good authority that Shakespeare 'had been in his younger years a Schoolmaster in the Countrey'.

Two of the most popular legends about Shakespeare refer to 'the missing years'. The first tells how he is supposed to have poached deer from the estate of Sir Thomas Lucy at Charlecote, near Stratford, was whipped, wrote an abusive ballad in revenge, and fled from home to escape Sir Thomas' wrath. The second tells how Shakespeare gained his entry to the theatrical profession by looking after the horses of rich theatregoers whilst they watched the performance.

A JEALOUS RIVAL

Both claims go back a long way, but modern research has cast grave doubts on their authenticity. All we know for certain about the missing years is that at some point after 1585 Shakespeare left home, went to London, joined a theatrical company, and began writing for the stage – although not necessarily in that order.

By 1592, when he was 28, Shakespeare must have been well known in his profession, for in that year the playwright Robert Greene wrote a pamphlet called *Greenes Groats-worth of Witte* in which he refers enviously to an 'upstart Crow' who fancies himself 'the onely Shake-scene in the country'. Greene parodied a line from *Henry VI* Part 3, so we know that Shakespeare had written at least part of this trilogy (generally regarded as his first surviving work) by this date.

Shakespeare's blossoming theatrical career was interrupted, however, by the plague, which closed down London's playhouses virtually completely

Stratford-upon-Avon
Shakespeare's home town was fairly small, but it had a splendid church and was the prosperous centre of a rich agricultural region. By the time of the 300th anniversary of Shakespeare's birth (above) it was becoming important for tourism.

New Place
By 1597 Shakespeare was affluent enough to buy New Place (below), the second largest house in Stratford. Standing in about an acre of ground, it had two barns and two orchards. The property was demolished in the 18th century and a garden (right) now occupies the site of the house.

from June 1592 to June 1594. During this period of enforced absence from the stage, Shakespeare turned to non-dramatic poetry, publishing *Venus and Adonis* in 1593 and *The Rape of Lucrece* in 1594. Both were dedicated to Henry Wriothesley, Third Earl of Southampton, who although extremely young (almost ten years younger than Shakespeare) was already well known for his generous patronage of literature.

In 1594 Shakespeare joined a new company, the (Lord) Chamberlain's Men, which soon became the leading theatrical group in London. It not only had the best writer, but also the best actors, its stars being Richard Burbage, as renowned in his own day as David Garrick or John Gielgud were to later ages, and Will Kempe, famous as a low comedian and dancer (in 1600 he morris-danced from London to Norwich for a bet).

The Chamberlain's Men made their first appearance at court at Christmas 1594, and payment was made jointly to Burbage, Kempe and Shakespeare – an indication of their prominence in the company. Shakespeare remained with the Chamberlain's Men (renamed the King's Men after the accession of James I in 1603) for the rest of his career. He was the only major writer of the time to have a permanent, prominent position with a team of first-class actors, and he often wrote parts with particular members of the company in mind. His own acting skills were valued by his colleagues (among the parts he is said to have played is the Ghost in *Hamlet*), but as he became busier as a writer and manager he had less time for acting, and

his last recorded performance was in a production of Ben Jonson's *Sejanus* in 1603.

By this time, Shakespeare, now approaching 40, had achieved great professional and financial success. In 1597 (a year after the death of his son Hamnet) he bought New Place, one of the finest houses in Stratford, and in 1602 (a year after the death of his father) he bought 127 acres of land there. The clearest indication of the reputation he enjoyed in the theatrical world is a passage in a literary handbook called *Palladis Tamia: Wit's Treasury* by Francis Meres, published in 1598: 'As Plautus and Seneca are accounted the best for Comedy and Tragedy among the Latines, so Shakespeare among the English is the most excellent in both kinds for the stage.'

EARLY RETIREMENT

In about 1610 Shakespeare left London and settled at his house in Stratford, where he lived the life of a retired gentleman. No-one knows why Shakespeare decided to leave the stage when he was still only in his mid-40s, but it has been suggested that he had suffered a severe illness. His first biographer, Nicholas Rowe, in his *Life* of 1709, wrote that Shakespeare spent his final years 'in ease, retirement, and the conversation of his friends'. He had family as well as friends to occupy him. His mother had died in 1608, but his wife and two daughters were still living. Susanna, the elder, married in 1607 and gave birth to a daughter the following year; Judith, the younger, married in February 1616.

Shakespeare was very dubious about his second son-in-law, Thomas Quiney, and with good reason. Not long before his marriage Quiney had made another woman pregnant, and a month after the wedding there was an unsavoury scandal when that woman died in childbirth. Two weeks later Shakespeare revised his will to try to ensure Judith a stable income if her feckless husband should leave her. A month later, on 23 April 1616 (on or about his 52nd birthday), Shakespeare died, and

Shakespeare's London
London in Elizabethan times was a thriving cosmopolitan city. The theatrical district was in the area of Southwark called Bankside (foreground in the engraving above).

Tribute in stone
The memorial bust of Shakespeare in Stratford church is shown being made in this later, romanticized painting (below).

two days afterwards was buried in the church in which he had been baptized. The cause of death is unknown, but John Ward, vicar of Stratford half a century later, wrote that 'Shakespear, Drayton [another playwright], and Ben Jhonson had a merry meeting, and itt seems drank too hard, for Shakespear died of a feavour there contracted.'

A memorial bust, showing the writer with pen and paper, was soon erected in the church, but the real monument to Shakespeare came a little later, with the publication of the first collected edition of his plays in 1623. Of the many tributes paid to Shakespeare, the one that his friend Ben Jonson wrote for this volume has never been bettered:
. . . I confess thy writings to be such,
As neither Man, nor Muse, can praise too much . . .
He was not of an age, but for all time!

SELECTED TRAGEDIES

Concerning aspects of love, honour, betrayal and vanity, *Romeo and Juliet*, *Hamlet* and *King Lear* are among the most enduring tragedies in world literature.

*K*ing *Lear*, *Hamlet* and *Romeo and Juliet* are three of Shakespeare's greatest plays and each one explores a different aspect of tragedy. *Lear* is the story of a world turned upside down by the actions of a vain old man who must then live through the consequences of his foolishness; *Hamlet* is a revenge play with a hero who cannot quite bring himself to play the part of valiant avenger; and *Romeo and Juliet* is a love story that ends in tragedy because of forces outside the lovers' control. All the plays were written for an Elizabethan audience who would have been familiar with the conventions and themes, but the plays are as moving and as powerful today as they were 400 years ago.

ROMEO AND JULIET

Romeo and Juliet is the most famous love story of all time. Several versions existed before Shakespeare and many have been written since. None, however, is so complex and sublime as Shakespeare's tragedy, which explores the nature of love and fate with a poetic intensity as passionate as the love between Romeo and Juliet.

GUIDE TO THE PLOT
The story is one of constant action, beginning with the fight between the feuding Capulets and Montagues, the two leading families in Verona. Romeo, a Montague, goes in disguise to a feast at the Capulet household, where his infatuation with Lord Capulet's niece Rosaline is forgotten as soon as he sets eyes on Capulet's daughter Juliet. Her aggressive cousin Tybalt threatens to kill Romeo immediately for being a Montague, but is prevented by Juliet's father, who wants to keep the peace.

Romeo leaves the Capulet feast with his friends Mercutio and Benvolio, but cannot bear to be parted from Juliet. He climbs over a wall into the garden and sees Juliet on her balcony. They declare their love for each other into the early hours of the morning, but realize the perils of their situation. Romeo goes to Friar Laurence to ask his help, and the Friar agrees to marry the young couple, hoping this will end the feud.

On his way back from the secret marriage, Romeo ignores a challenge from Tybalt to a duel, but Mercutio rushes in and is fatally wounded. Enraged by the death of his friend, Romeo kills Tybalt and is told he is to be banished from Verona. Despairing, but more deeply in love than ever, the lovers resort to desperate measures to see each other again.

Declaration of love
After a feast at the Capulet household, Romeo is overcome by the image of Juliet. Hastily he returns to her house, climbs over a garden wall and catches sight of his beloved on the balcony (left): "It is my lady; O, it is my love!" he gasps.

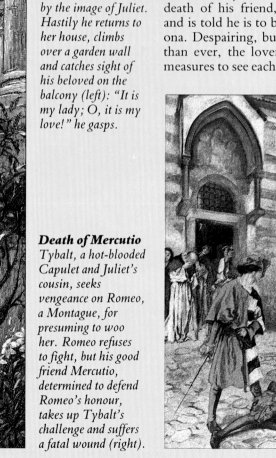

Death of Mercutio
Tybalt, a hot-blooded Capulet and Juliet's cousin, seeks vengeance on Romeo, a Montague, for presuming to woo her. Romeo refuses to fight, but his good friend Mercutio, determined to defend Romeo's honour, takes up Tybalt's challenge and suffers a fatal wound (right).

Fate is against Romeo and Juliet. Their happiness lies beyond their control, for they are born into families filled with mutual hatred. It is these "Two households, both alike in dignity" who unleash the tragedy, so blind are they in their prejudice. Set in this context, the story of Romeo and Juliet takes on a deeper sig-

John Pettie: Juliet and Friar Laurence. With permission of the Governors of the Royal Shakespeare Theatre

nificance; their tragedy is the price that must be paid before the "ancient grudge" between the Montagues and Capulets can be forgotten.

STAR-CROSSED LOVERS

It is the lovers, however, not the families, who are the focus of the drama. In charting the swift progress of their love during the brief time they know each other, Shakespeare draws on his matchless richness of imagery to convey an ideal state of love that is filled with romance, sexual longing, fear, trepidation and poignancy. Each is the other's centre; outside claims mean nothing in the force of their love. Juliet longs to escape the confines of their family feud: "Deny thy father and refuse thy name . . . And I'll no longer be a Capulet." Within hours of meeting Romeo, she tells him: "My bounty is as boundless as the sea,/My love as deep; the more I give to thee,/The more I have, for both are infinite."

Their love may be infinite, but it is

shortlived. It is almost as if their ecstasy is too sweet and too bright to flourish in such an imperfect world. Their awareness of the perils they face adds a "sweet sorrow" to their love, which turns to a desperate passion as their circumstances worsen. Friar Laurence predicted:
"*These violent delights have violent ends . . .*
Therefore, love moderately: long love doth so;
Too swift arrives as tardy as too slow."
And Romeo himself was fearful moments before he met Juliet that fateful night: "for my mind misgives/Some consequence, yet hanging in the stars . . ." His words quickly gather a prophetic meaning.

It is the malevolent stars that Romeo seeks to thwart in the end. Sick of being "fortune's fool", he shouts "then I defy you, stars!", as he sets off to decide his own fate. But it has already been determined, and so this "pair of star-cross'd lovers" continue with "The fearful passage of their death-mark'd love."

> "*. . . but come what sorrow can,/*
> *It cannot countervail the exchange*
> *of joy/That one short minute*
> *gives me in her sight.*"
>
> ROMEO

Henry Stacey Marks: The Apothecary/Fine Art Photographic Library

Friar Laurence
Grief-stricken at her separation from Romeo, Juliet begs Friar Laurence (left) to come to her rescue once again.

Fatal potion
Romeo, on learning of Juliet's tragic death, vows that he will 'sleep' with her that night. He exhorts a poor apothecary (top right) to concoct "a dram of poison" such that "the life-weary taker may fall dead".

Tragic awakening
Juliet wakes (right) to find Romeo at her side, poisoned, his lips still warm, and groans that "no friendly drop" remains for her to swallow.

Ferdinand Piloty: Romeo & Juliet. With permission of the Governors of the Royal Shakespeare Theatre

HAMLET

Hamlet is the most famous and most quoted of Shakespeare's works, and has a good claim to be considered the most popular – as well as fascinating – play ever written. It combines marvellous poetry and unforgettable characters, and although it has great tragic power, it is also among the wittiest and most exciting of Shakespeare's plays. For sheer theatrical entertainment it is unrivalled, and the part of Hamlet – enormously demanding physically and intellectually – is one of the supreme tests of the actor's art.

In the gripping opening scenes the play promises to be a straightforward revenge tragedy, but it soon develops into a far more intricate and involved study of human motives. The many unanswered questions in the plot simply add to the imaginative complexity of the story. For every question we might want to ask Hamlet, he is asking much deeper questions on moral and philosophical issues.

GUIDE TO THE PLOT

Hamlet is a story of a son's revenge for his father's death. Hamlet, Prince of Denmark, is bewildered and unhappy following his father's death and his mother's marriage to his uncle Claudius after an indecently short time of mourning. Hamlet's sense of foreboding is transformed into horror when his father's ghost

Mary Evans Picture Library

Enter the ghost
Confronted with his father's ghost on the battlements, Hamlet is horrified to learn that his uncle Claudius is his father's assassin. "If thou didst ever thy dear father love", the ghost entreats, "Revenge his foul and most unnatural murder."

Dramatic evidence
A troupe of actors inspires Hamlet to test Claudius – he will stage a play before the royal household (below). In the story a king is poisoned, and Hamlet intends to study Claudius' response – "The play's the thing / Wherein I'll catch the conscience of the king." His plan works, as Claudius does indeed betray himself.

Daniel Maclise: Hamlet and the players. Roy Miles Fine Paintings/ Bridgeman Art Library

appears and tells him that he did not die of natural causes, but was poisoned by Claudius. The Ghost urges Hamlet to avenge his death.

Hamlet feigns madness and Claudius becomes worried by his strange behaviour. He sends for Rosencrantz and Guildenstern, two of Hamlet's old friends, to spy on the young prince. A group of players arrive at the court and at Hamlet's request perform a play about a man who commits murder to become king. Hamlet is convinced of his uncle's guilt when Claudius rushes out of the audience before the play is over.

In spite of the evidence Hamlet still delays revenge, and Claudius has time to despatch his nephew to England. Just before his departure, Hamlet accidentally kills Polonius, adviser to the King. Hamlet himself then becomes the object of revenge – for Laertes, Polonius' son. And

> "To be, or not to be: that is the question:/Whether 'tis nobler in the mind to suffer/The slings and arrows of outrageous fortune,/Or to take arms against a sea of troubles…"
>
> HAMLET

so the play moves towards a bloody climax.

Hamlet promises the Ghost that he will revenge "his foul and most unnatural murder". In fact, for most of the play he conspicuously fails to do so, wishing it was not his responsibility: "The time is out of joint: O cursed spite, / That ever I was born to set it right!" Miserable, frustrated and overwhelmed with disgust for life itself, he retreats not just from the act of vengeance but from the whole burden of living.

THE RELUCTANT HERO

Hamlet knows "Something is rotten in the state of Denmark", but consistently shirks confrontation, hiding instead in books, depression and soliloquy, imagining the relief that death would bring:

"To die: to sleep;
No more; and by a sleep to say we end
The heart-ache, and the thousand natural
                              shocks
That flesh is heir to."

The corruption he sees everywhere makes Hamlet a reluctant lover. He describes his mother's marriage bed as "Stew'd in corruption, honeying and making love / Over the nasty sty", and abuses his sweetheart Ophelia: "Get thee to a nunnery, why wouldst thou be a breeder of sinners?"

Filled with doubt and world-weariness, he asks: "What is a man,/If his chief good and market of his time/Be but to sleep and feed? a beast, no more."

Seeking to live in a world of beauty, Hamlet finds only "an unweeded garden/That grows to seed; things rank and gross in nature." Aspiring to virtue, Hamlet hates the deed he must perform and then hates himself for delaying. It is only when events overtake him that he finds himself – reluctantly – forced into action.

Innocent victim
Epitomizing purity and goodness, Ophelia (left) is one of the casualties of Hamlet's quest for vengeance. Her love for him survives his cruelty, but the sudden and senseless murder of her father finally tips the balance of her mind. She kills herself – drowning, bedecked in flowers, "in the weeping brook".

The funeral
Ophelia's funeral (below) is a sombre, grief-ridden affair, with Laertes cursing the wrong done to "her fair and unpolluted flesh" by Hamlet.

Paul Albert Steck. Ophelia. Musée du Petit Palais, Paris/Giraudon/Bridgeman Art Library

Mary Evans Picture Library

17

KING LEAR

King Lear is the most overwhelming of Shakespeare's tragedies, exploring vast themes of kingship, filial love, madness and evil, in a setting of ancient Britain.

The extremes of emotion and human understanding that are explored in the story were once thought too painful, and for more than 150 years the play was performed only in a mutilated version with a happy ending. Some critics have even thought that the play is 'unactable' – too harrowing to be performed successfully – but Shakespeare did not write his play simply to be read. It takes a great actor in the title role to bring *King Lear* fully to life, but it then can offer a theatrical experience of incomparable pathos.

GUIDE TO THE PLOT

Lear is 80 years old when the play opens, and tired of kingship. He decides to divide his kingdom among his three daughters, giving the largest share to the one who can profess she loves him the most. But Cordelia, his youngest and favourite daughter, cannot bring herself to barter her love for material profit. She says nothing, and is banished from the kingdom. Goneril and Regan soon tire of providing hospitality to their father and his noisy retinue. Unable to bear their

> *"Pray, do not mock me:/ I am a very foolish fond old man . . ."*
>
> LEAR

ingratitude, Lear disappears one stormy night with his Fool. Stripped of everything, he begins to realize the folly of his action. His sanity cracks, but in his weakened and humbled state he acquires compassion and understanding.

Ford Madox Brown: Cordelia's Portion. National Museums and Galleries on Merseyside (Lady Lever Art Gallery)

Dividing Britain
(above) Tired of the responsibilities of monarchy and ready to "unburthen'd crawl toward death", Lear summons his three daughters, intending to divide the kingdom among them according to their love for him.

"Blow, winds!"
Lear, battling against the elements and raging against his two "unnatural" daughters, struggles to hold on to his sanity – "In such a night/To shut me out! Pour on; I will endure . . ."

J. Runciman: King Lear in the Storm. National Gallery of Scotland

Mary Evans Picture Library

Filial love
Knowing how her sisters have abused her father, Cordelia forgets her own grievances in her compassion for his plight (left).

The final blow
Too late, Edmund repents. Cordelia is executed and Lear, grief-stricken, dies with her in his arms (below).

More sinn'd against than sinning." There, under the wild elements, an extraordinary trio of madness is enacted.

These tense, powerful scenes of passion form the centre of the drama. Lear's insights into the inescapable tragedy of humanity on "this great stage of fools" are linked with the Fool's satirical comments and Edgar's feigned ravings. Lear is quite mad at the point when he sees Edgar, disguised as a beggar with nothing but a blanket as clothing. "Hast thou given all to thy two daughters?" he asks pitifully. When Lear appears later in the play it is to be reunited with Cordelia. He feels he is emerging "out o' the grave", and

The sub-plot, also involving a father and his children, is woven through the main story to great effect. Gloucester makes a judgement as mistaken as Lear's by rejecting his good son Edgar in favour of his ambitious, scheming 'bastard' son Edmund. Edmund unites with Goneril and Regan in his quest for power. The sisters are rivals in greed and in their desire for Edmund.

MADNESS

A central theme running throughout the play is madness. Lear's initial act of dividing his kingdom would have seemed insane to contemporary audiences. The

James Barry: King Lear weeping over the body of Cordelia. Tate Gallery, London

---

In the Background

DUAL KINGSHIP

King *Lear* was performed before James, King of England and Scotland, when he was seeking the union of the two countries, wanting them to 'be joined in a perpetual marriage'. Although this took another century to achieve, Lear's madness in dividing up his kingdom would have fuelled James' cause.

James I, after John de Critz the Elder (detail). National Portrait Gallery, London

---

chaos arising from the break-up of society and threat to world order is seen as a natural sequence. Lear also pays for his folly in banishing Cordelia, the only daughter who loves him. He is left to learn of the cruel hypocrisy of Goneril and Regan and to realize "How sharper than a serpent's tooth it is / To have a thankless child!" His disbelief and outrage that they should want to humiliate and impoverish him leave him almost speechless:
"I will have such revenges on you both
That all the world shall – I will do such
things, –
What they are, yet I know not. . ."
"O Fool, I shall go mad!" says Lear, even as he reflects on the nature of authority and power, and on those who have nothing. Out on the heath Lear competes with the storm in his fury and feels his punishment is too great: "I am a man/

scarcely recognizes her – but only she has the power to heal his stricken senses.

Similarly, Gloucester, who admits to being "almost mad myself", undergoes horrific punishment at the hands of Regan and her husband. He is blinded, but he develops a spiritual insight from his blindness: "I have no way and therefore want no eyes;/I stumbled when I saw."

Lear rises above himself through his suffering. His violent and rash temper, his inflated vanity and poor judgement have been replaced with love and humility. Purged by the storm and madness, he is able to describe himself as he is:
"Pray, do not mock me:
I am a very foolish fond old man,
Fourscore and upward, not an hour more or
less;
And, to deal plainly,
I fear I am not in my perfect mind."

CHARACTERS IN FOCUS

A genius for creating characters steeped in pyschological complexity, Shakespeare has moved and fascinated audiences the world over. His heroes are impetuous, misguided or vacillating on a grand scale. They are tragic because their heroism is combined with human weakness, their capacity for destruction with intelligence and imagination.

WHO'S WHO
ROMEO AND JULIET

Romeo	A young, impassioned Montague, who falls in love with the 'forbidden' Juliet.
Juliet	A Capulet, she is willing to renounce her family for her new-found love.
Friar Laurence	Romeo's wise mentor, who helps unite the lovers.
Mercutio	Romeo's close friend and ally, quick to preserve Montague honour.

KING LEAR

King Lear	The ageing, capricious monarch who precipitates his own tragic destiny.
Cordelia	Lear's youngest daughter whose honesty loses her her inheritance.
Goneril	The eldest daughter, she is clever, lustful, iron-willed and voraciously ambitious.
Regan	The brutal and vindictive second sister, she rivals Goneril in her desire for power.

HAMLET

Hamlet	The young Prince of Denmark who agonizes over his father's death.
Claudius	Hamlet's uncle, now stepfather, who comes to the throne by dubious means.
Ophelia	Hamlet's sweetheart, she is the innocent victim of his see-sawing emotions. She loses first her mind and then her life.
Gertrude	Hamlet's mother, a "most seeming-virtuous queen" who remarries with undignified haste.

ROMEO AND JULIET

Just 13 years old, the beautiful Juliet (above) shows a resolve and wisdom beyond her years. Undeterred by her family's opposition to Romeo, she marries him in secret. Later, with the help of Friar Laurence she devises a desperate plan, knowing that it is the only way she can be united with her lover. "Love give me strength! and strength shall help afford."

"As gentle as a lamb", Romeo (right) is nevertheless capable of violence when love and loyalty are at stake. But it does not come naturally, and although he willingly risks his life to cast his eyes on his beloved, he is reluctant to fight a duel with Juliet's kinsman Tybalt. "O sweet Juliet", he cries out, "Thy beauty hath made me effeminate,/ And in my temper soften'd valour's steel!" He does fight Tybalt, however, and suffers the consequences, ultimately pushed to the point of suicide rather than accepting life without his love.

HAMLET

[Th]e encounter between Hamlet and the spirit of [his] father (right) provides a painful confirmation [of] Hamlet's worst imaginings – his noble father [wa]s murdered, and "The serpent that did sting thy [fat]her's life/Now wears his crown." Reluctantly, [Ha]mlet recognizes his duty to "Revenge his foul [an]d most unnatural murder." A soldier, scholar [an]d philosopher, he is riven by inner conflict: shall [he] give up this earthly life, the "sea of troubles . . . [th]e heart-ache, and the thousand natural shocks/ [th]at flesh is heir to", or choose the path of [ho]nourable action?

KING LEAR

[Ge]ntle Cordelia's love for her father (below) is not [suf]ficient to stave off Lear's tragic downfall. Vanity [ma]kes the ageing Lear prefer the flattery of his [tw]o heartless daughters to Cordelia's quieter [aff]irmations of obedience, love and honour. ["B]etter thou/Hadst not been born than not to have [ple]ased me better" a wounded, wilful Lear retorts. [Su]ffering brings him insight and humility, but [un]hinges his mind. It is in this state that Cordelia [fin]ds him, maltreated by her sisters and ravaged by [the] elements: "Had you not been their father, these [wh]ite flakes/Had challenged pity of them. Was this [a f]ace/To be opposed against the warring winds?" [Th]eir reunion heals their rift, but proves tragically [bri]ef.

Eugène Delacroix: Scene from Hamlet/Fotomas Index

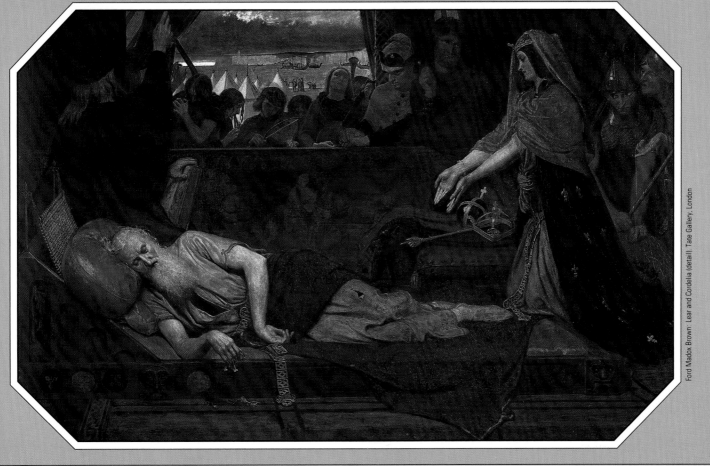

Ford Madox Brown: Lear and Cordelia (detail). Tate Gallery, London

A UNIVERSE OF FEELING

Famed for the breadth and power of his vision, Shakespeare penetrated the hidden recesses of the human spirit, lending grandeur to frailty and dignity to suffering.

William Shakespeare was above all else a man of the theatre, living a busy professional life that deeply influenced what and how he wrote. Relatively early in his career he became a full-time member of a company of players, the (Lord) Chamberlain's Men. He acted with them, wrote his plays for them to perform, and quickly became a shareholder in what proved to be their thriving concern. There is every reason to suppose that, as 'writer in residence', he adapted himself to the needs of the company, tailoring the parts he created to the available talent; for example, it can hardly be a coincidence that the role of fool, or jester, became more sophisticated in plays such as *As You Like It, Twelfth Night* and *King Lear,* written after the gifted Robert Armin joined the Chamberlain's Men.

"A MUSE OF FIRE"

Shakespeare must have been involved in all the important phases of a production, and wrote with an exact knowledge of what could and could not be done on the Elizabethan stage. One of his many skills was to make words substitute for elaborate and convincing stage properties, not only setting the scene, but generating the atmosphere of a place and time in order to transport the spectator to the Forest of Arden, for example, or the cities of Verona or Alexandria.

A writer in Shakespeare's situation needed to be able to provide copy whenever it was required, without waiting months for possible inspiration. One of the few facts that we know about his writing habits is that he was extraordinarily fluent. His fellow-actors Heminge and Condell prefaced their posthumous collections of his plays by recalling that 'His mind and hand went together: and what he thought, he uttered with that easiness, that we have scarce received from him a blot in his papers.'

In a career lasting about 25 years, Shakespeare is generally accepted as having written 36 plays, as well as collaborating late in life with John Fletcher on *Henry VIII, The Two Noble Kinsmen* and a lost work, *Cardenio.* He seems to have worked as a collaborator less often than the majority of his contemporaries, but part of his professional work certainly involved adapting or improving plays by other hands; one of these, *Sir Thomas More,* includes a three-page insertion that is possibly in Shakespeare's own hand.

As well as receiving a standard grammar-school education, Shakespeare read widely and turned what he read to professional use. He found many of his plots in the Italian and French short stories that Elizabethan Englishmen were busy translating. For his Roman plays – *Julius Caesar, Antony and Cleopatra, Coriolanus* – he drew on Sir Thomas North's translation of the ancient Greek philosopher and

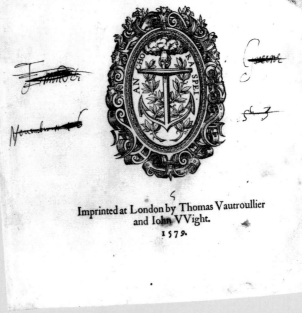

THE LIVES OF THE NOBLE GRECIANS AND ROMANES, COMPARED together by that graue learned Philosopher and Historiographer, Plutarke of Chæronea:

Translated out of Greeke into French by IAMES AMYOT, Abbot of Bellozane, Bishop of Auxerre, one of the Kings priuy counsel, and great Amner of Fraunce, and out of French into Englishe, by Thomas North.

Imprinted at London by Thomas Vautroullier and Iohn VVight. 1579.

Bodleian Library, Oxford. vet. A1 c22/Weidenfeld Archive

Elizabethan Rome
Shakespeare drew on Sir Thomas North's translation (left) of Plutarch's Greek and Roman biographies. While exploiting such classical devices as rhetoric in brilliant speeches like Mark Antony's oration, he painted a distinctly Elizabethan 'Rome' with its anachronistic striking clock and its band of conspirators wearing "their hats pluck'd about their ears".

Her Majesty's pleasure
Shakespeare very probably performed in his own and others' plays in the presence of Queen Elizabeth (right). His work contains thinly veiled eulogies to her, and his history plays endorse her and her predecessors' right to the throne. Patronage naturally secured its quota of apposite compliments.

historian Plutarch, in many places following North's text very closely – adding just the few significant master-touches needed to convert eloquent prose into magnificent dramatic verse. The factual basis for Shakespeare's English histories was supplied by two standard authorities, Holinshed and Hall, but the plots of *Hamlet* and *King Lear* were taken over from several older versions.

An examination of Shakespeare's sources highlights the expertise with which he adapted stories and characters for the stage. He eliminated, expanded and reshaped his material in the interests of dramatic effectiveness and also, without doubt, to express his own feelings, thoughts and preoccupations. One among many possible examples is his treatment of *Othello*, originally a rather sordid little tale of lust and murder. Shakespeare transformed this story by adding to the stature of both Iago – enigmatic and heaven-defying in his malignancy – and the noble-hearted but distracted Moor whom he dupes.

But perhaps the clearest evidence of Shakespeare's skill lies in his manipulation of the sub-plots which serve such important functions in his plays, whether pro-

By permission of the Trustees of the Will of the late Lord Berkeley/Courtauld Institute of Art/Weidenfeld

A new patron
(above) After the closure of theatres, Shakespeare joined the Lord Chamberlain's Men under the patronage of Lord Hunsdon.

Playhouses
Most of Shakespeare's plays were performed in the Globe Theatre (right), described as the 'wooden O' because of its circular shape.

viding a contrast to the main action or intertwining with it. In *Henry IV*, Shakespeare's introduction of Falstaff – one of his supreme inventions – serves brilliantly to juxtapose comic low-life junketings and intrigues with the more solemn and deadly manoeuvres of feudal magnates. And in his *King Lear*, Shakespeare fuses mythical British history chronicled in the older play *(King Leir)* with a new story – that of Gloucester, which he took from an episode in Sir Philip Sidney's pastoral romance *Arcadia* (1590).

As a man of the theatre, Shakespeare intended his writing to be at its most effective in performance, and to be widely popular. He exploited (though he also doubtless shared) sentiments such as patriotism, which are given rousing expression in the big set-pieces of *Henry V* and *King John,* and he aimed to please both his

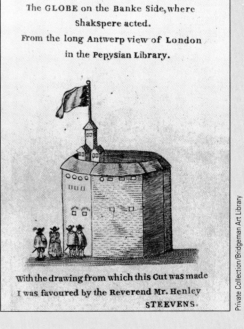

The GLOBE on the Banke Side, where Shakspere acted.

From the long Antwerp view of London in the Pepysian Library.

With the drawing from which this Cut was made I was favoured by the Reverend Mr. Henley
STEEVENS.

Private Collection/Bridgeman Art Library

audiences and those in authority: *Richard III,* portraying its subject as a monster, was safely loyal propaganda on behalf of the established Tudor regime which had replaced Richard and the Yorkists.

The unusual setting of a later play, *Macbeth,* was clearly prompted by the fact that the English throne was by this time occupied by a Scot in the person of the Stuart King James I, who was also a generous patron of Shakespeare's company. James' supposed ancestor, Banquo, is displayed to advantage in the tragedy, and for good measure Shakespeare works in a tableau of all the Stuart kings before James, in whom, implicitly, the line gloriously culminates.

Shakespeare also accommodated himself to literary fashions, although with

Charles Cattermole: Shakespeare acting before Queen Elizabeth. With permission of the Governors of the Royal Shakespeare Theatre

Playing the Palace
The Chamberlain's Men put on two plays at Greenwich Palace (above) during Christmas 1594.

Deathless print
Individual plays were published in Shakespeare's lifetime, King Lear *(below) appearing in 1608.*

readers and spectators have felt that Shakespeare's personal emotions must underlie the great tragedies of the 1600s – the all-encompassing blackness of *Macbeth,* the sense of sexual disgust in *Hamlet,* and the mind-breaking verbal storms of *Lear.* If this is so, the mellow mood of Shakespeare's last plays – romances or tragi-comedies – may be equally significant, representing a personal recovery. But it is also true that this type of play had become popular, so even here it is impossible to separate the private from the public man.

In his sonnets, Shakespeare complained of the fate that made him a showman – 'a motley to the view' – instead of a gentleman-poet. But although only 18 of his plays were published during his lifetime, this does not signify indifference to the survival of his dramatic work: it was not then customary to publish collections. Shakespeare was – contrary to popular belief – well known in his own time. As early as 1598 a commentator said, 'Shakespeare among the English is the most excellent in both kinds [comedy and tragedy] for the stage'. He became the premier playwright of a theatrical company whose pre-eminence was recognized in 1603, when it ceased to be the Lord Chamberlain's and was taken into royal protection.

LATER PRAISE

Seven years after his death, two of his fellow-players, John Heminge and Henry Condell, published a collection of 36 of his plays, prefaced by the enthusiastic verses of (among others) Shakespeare's younger friend and rival Ben Jonson, who hailed him as 'The applause, delight, the wonder of our Stage!'

But for the initiative taken by Heminge and Condell, half of Shakespeare's output as a dramatist would have been lost forever. In their book – now known everywhere as 'the First Folio' – they express a wish which now seems something of an understatement: 'to keep the memory of so worthy a friend and fellow alive, as was our Shakespeare'.

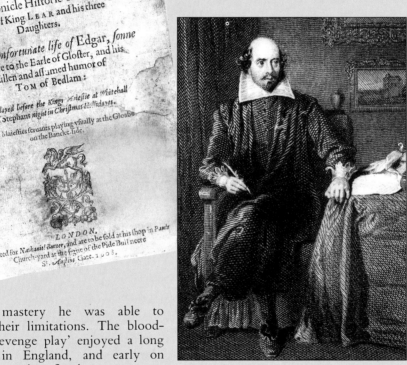

increasing mastery he was able to transcend their limitations. The blood-spattered 'revenge play' enjoyed a long popularity in England, and early on Shakespeare made a flamboyant attempt to outdo his rivals by piling horror on horror in *Titus Andronicus.* By contrast, *Hamlet,* some ten years later, maintains the form of the revenge play while operating on a subtler psychological level and questioning the validity of revenge.

Only in this indirect fashion can Shakespeare's personal outlook be inferred. Perhaps the most fundamental conviction in his work is that civil strife and the breakdown of order are the worst of evils – a conviction understandable in an age of assassinations, rebellions and ideological conflicts. Moreover, many

How many more?
We know at least one play by Shakespeare (above) was lost without trace. Were there others?

Early graphics
This scene from Titus Andronicus *(right), c. 1594, is the earliest extant Shakespearean illustration.*

The greatest of all English writers, Shakespeare was brilliantly gifted both as poet and playwright. By the early 1590s he was an accomplished writer of history plays as well as the creator of several lyrical comedies. His first major tragedy, *Romeo and Juliet,* has this same quality of lyricism. Gradually, the comedies became more psychologically acute and dramatic, while his histories expanded to create a panorama of the recent English past.

Around the turn of the century Shakespeare began to write his most sublime tragedies and darkest comedies. In *Hamlet* the Elizabethan 'revenge tragedy' is converted into a profound, enigmatic psychological study. In *Othello* the tragic hero's flaw is jealousy, in *King Lear* it is vanity, and in *Macbeth* ambition. Shakespeare ended his dazzling career with a series of 'romances' including *The Tempest*, in which the lasting note is one of reconciliation.

Sir John Everett Millais: The Princes in the Tower (detail). Royal Holloway and Bedford New College/Bridgeman Art Library

RICHARD III

✦ c.1592 ✦

Innocent children of royal blood (left) are the ultimate victims of an irredeemable villain in this study of malice. Richard, Duke of Gloucester, crooked in body and mind, detests the "weak, piping time of peace" that follows a Yorkist victory in the Wars of the Roses. He is also seethingly envious of his oldest brother, now King Edward IV. Delighting in his own manipulative powers, he woos a woman whose betrothed he has just killed, plots the murder of his brother Clarence and, when Edward dies, persuades Londoners to set aside the young heirs (whom he also murders) and proclaim him King. But his tyranny encourages rebellion, and one last battle is fought at Bosworth Field.

HENRY IV PARTS 1 AND 2

✦ c.1597 ✦

As heir apparent, Prince Hal incurs kingly disapproval for his friendship with the gross, rascally Falstaff (below). Hal's father, King Henry IV, has usurped the throne and his hold on it is uncertain. Northumberland and Worcester rise in open rebellion, along with Northumberland's warrior son, Harry Hotspur. Meanwhile, Hal seems content to consort with Falstaff and his cronies at the Boar's Head Tavern, and even takes part in a robbery. In reality, however, the Prince has every intention of reforming when the time comes. In *Henry IV* Part 2, a new conspiracy is suppressed, Hal becomes King, and Falstaff tries – disastrously – to capitalize on their old acquaintance.

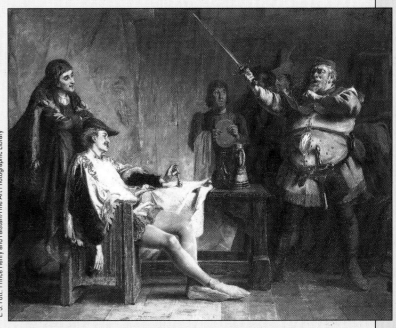

L. J. Pott: Prince Henry and Falstaff/Fine Art Photographic Library

25

OTHELLO

✦ c.1603 ✦

Othello the Moor woos Desdemona with stories of his adventures (above) and she marries him despite their differences of race and age. Her father protests, but since Othello is an able general in the service of Venice, he is overruled by the senate. Othello is sent, with the senate's blessing, to deal with a crisis in the Venetian colony of Cyprus, and Desdemona joins him there. But Othello's ensign, Iago, implicates his rival, Cassio, as Desdemona's lover. He insidiously pours false evidence of Desdemona's infidelity into the ears of a distracted Othello. There follows a night of terrible violence which ends in tragedy for all.

JULIUS CAESAR

✦ c.1599 ✦

Republicans driven to desperate measures by Caesar's growing egotism, assassinate him (below) on the inauspicious Ides of March. At first the conspirators win public support for their coup: the leader, Brutus, is a man of utter integrity. But his very high-mindedness blinds him to political realities, and Caesar's closest friend and follower, Mark Antony, is able to sway Rome's citizens with his masterly oratory, inviting them to "let slip the dogs of war". The republicans flee and raise an army. Dreams (or visions) which were at first a source of terrible premonition to Caesar now haunt Brutus as he awaits the battle.

MACBETH
◆ c.1605 ◆

Macbeth, a Scottish nobleman, fresh from battle in the service of his king, is hailed by three witches (right) who prophesy that he will become Thane of Cawdor and "king hereafter". The first prophecy comes true immediately, which makes the possibility of his becoming king seem credible. Disturbed and tempted, Macbeth confides the news to his ambitious wife, at whose urging he murders King Duncan. He throws the blame on Duncan's sons who flee to England.

Macbeth becomes King, but this glory is accompanied by tormenting fears and doubts. Recalling the witches' prophecy that Banquo, and not he, would father a line of kings, Macbeth hires assassins to kill Banquo and his only son, Fleance. The bloody scheme is thwarted when Fleance escapes. Banquo's ghost returns to haunt Macbeth, terrifying and incriminating him in front of his dinner guests. Lady Macbeth, though seemingly ruthless and contemptuous of signs of weakness in her husband, descends into madness.

In a futile search for security, Macbeth wades ever deeper in blood. The English forces invade, supporting the cause of Duncan's son Malcolm. Deserted and at bay, Macbeth clings to the witches' ostensibly reassuring prophecy that he will suffer no defeat "Till Burnam wood remove to Dunsinane . . ."

ANTONY AND CLEOPATRA
◆ c.1606 ◆

Ill-fated love and death on an epic scale (left) are the substance of this account of events that follow the story of *Julius Caesar*. The triumvirate of Mark Antony, Octavius and Lepidus has taken control of the Roman world. But Antony, ruling the eastern Empire, becomes besotted with Cleopatra, Queen of Egypt, whose dangerous fascination destroys his energy and judgement. Away from her influence, he strengthens his political position by marrying Octavius' sister. But while the prudent, calculating Octavius continues to consolidate his own power (by dispensing with Lepidus), Antony succumbs once more to Cleopatra. He alienates Octavius personally, politically and beyond repair.

War breaks out between Rome and its eastern Empire. At the decisive Battle of Actium, Cleopatra's ships take flight at the critical moment and Antony deserts his fleet to follow her. In Alexandria, the lovers are separated. But they are of one mind in deciding how to seal their extraordinary love.

The scale of the concept and the splendour of the language elevate the lovers' passion to such grandeur that when they vacate their empire of love, "there is nothing left remarkable/Beneath the visiting moon."

The Elizabethan Theatre

During Shakespeare's lifetime some actors advanced from being mere 'strolling players' – little better than vagabonds – to respected professionals who even performed at court.

The theatrical environment that nourished Shakespeare's genius had all the vigour and freshness of youth, for it had begun within his own lifetime. Throughout the Middle Ages, plays had normally been local and amateur productions – often of considerable artistry – which dealt with biblical subjects and were performed to celebrate saints' days and other holy days. When, with the 16th-century Protestant Reformation, the saints' days disappeared, the old plays were suppressed as religiously and politically suspect. Religious topics were officially banned from the stage. As a result the Elizabethan – and Shakespearean – drama became strikingly secular, with love, lust, ambition and murder becoming the dramatist's chief preoccupations.

THE FIRST THEATRE

The suppression of the amateur tradition gave the professionals their opportunity. Troupes of 'players' had already been in existence for a century or more. Until the 1570s they worked as 'strolling players', continually on the move and performing in places such as guildhalls and inn courtyards. Their status was not far removed from that of vagrants. The players' only protection was to attach themselves to a noble patron who would allow them to become his 'men' and wear his livery, thus guaranteeing them an income as well as ridding them of the stigma of being 'masterless'. If the noble was a royal favourite, like the Earl of Leicester, his 'men' might be given the opportunity to appear before the court; but at other times their patron was only too pleased if the players continued to 'stroll' rather than be entirely dependent on his bounty. Powerful patronage remained essential even after the players built their own theatres, and all the great Elizabethan companies were somebody's men – the Lord Chamberlain's, the Lord High Admiral's, the Earl of Worcester's, for example.

Companies of players are known to have hired halls in London early in Elizabeth I's reign, but their conquest of the city did not begin until 1574, when Shakespeare was already 10 years old. In this year the Queen allowed Leicester's Men to perform regularly in the city on weekdays. Two years later their leader, James Burbage, took a 21-year lease on some ground at Shoreditch and built Eng-

land's first playhouse, known simply as the Theatre. Almost simultaneously an enterprising schoolmaster started a rather different venture in Blackfriars, using his pupils as performers. And in Shoreditch the Theatre soon had a rival and neighbour in the Curtain.

Playhouses obviously satisfied a demand, but there were never more than a handful in London and one or two in the provinces, since drama had powerful enemies. Puritanism was already at work in English life, and its influence made the City fathers hostile to plays and players – so much so that Elizabethan theatres were built in places where the authorities had no jurisdiction: in 'liberties' such as London's Shoreditch, or just across the Thames on Bankside in Southwark, among the bear gardens (where the popular pastime of bear-baiting took place), and in brothels.

It was to Bankside that James Burbage's son, Richard, moved the Theatre in 1599, when its lease ran out. The building was dismantled, timber by timber, reassembled on the other side of the river, and renamed the Globe. This is where most of Shakespeare's greatest works received their first performance.

The City fathers closed the playhouses whenever they could find an excuse. During outbreaks of plague they claimed, not unreasonably, that playhouses constituted health hazards. The worst outbreak closed the theatres for two years from 1592 to 1594.

The court and the aristocracy were generally more sympathetic to the players than the City

Noble patron
Robert Dudley (above), Earl of Leicester, a favourite of Elizabeth I, had his own company of actors.

Bloody entertainment
Bear-baiting (left), bull-baiting and cock-fighting were immensely popular in the 16th century. Acting was initially part of the same disreputable world.

Mary Evans Picture Library

Inn-yard drama

(above and right) Before the establishment of permanent theatres in London, plays were acted in public halls and private houses, but above all in inn-yards. The typical layout of the yards provided a ready-made arena and galleries for spectators, and landlords welcomed the additional trade.

The Swan Theatre

(left) This drawing, a copy of one made by Johannes de Witt, a Dutchman who visited London in 1596, is the only known contemporary view of the interior of an Elizabethan theatre. De Witt described the Swan (which was newly opened at the time) as 'the largest and most magnificent' of London's theatres, 'for it accommodates in its seats three thousand persons, and is built of a mass of flint stones . . . and supported by wooden columns painted in such excellent imitation of marble that it is able to deceive even the most cunning'. More commonly theatres were made entirely of wood. This was a fire hazard – and indeed the Globe burned down in 1613.

fathers, but tight control was still exercised over the plays. Every script had to be submitted to a court official, the Master of the Revels, for vetting, and in 1605 the unlicensed performance of *Eastward Hoe!*, a comedy containing uncomplimentary remarks about the Scots, led to a wholesale shake-up of the player companies, which were forcibly amalgamated into three and put under the patronage (and control) of the Privy Council.

Despite all these hazards, there was money to be made in the theatre by those leading members owning shares in the companies. The most successful were the Lord Chamberlain's Men, run by the Burbages, and the Admiral's Men, effectively controlled by Philip Henslowe. Henslowe was a hard-as-nails businessman whose diverse interests included pawnbroking, bear-baiting and brothels. Shakespeare worked for the Lord Chamberlain's Men, where Richard Burbage established himself as a great actor in such roles as Richard III, Hamlet, King Lear and Othello. Burbage's only rival on the Elizabethan stage was the Admiral's Edward Alleyn, who took the lead in the plays of their own outstanding writer, Christopher Marlowe. Alleyn was shrewd enough to marry Henslowe's step-daughter, thus joining the management. He became very rich and respectable, founding the famous school Dulwich College.

Competition between these leading companies was fierce. When Shakespeare wrote a play featuring a rascally fat knight named Sir John Oldcastle, objections from the descendants of Oldcastle – a real person – forced him to change the character's name to Falstaff. Henslowe and the Admiral's men quickly jumped into the fray, commissioning a new piece, *Sir John Oldcastle,* to give a 'true and honourable history' of the knight as a counter to Shakespeare's 'forged invention'. An alternative method of dealing with a rival's successful play was to pirate it – a possibility that deterred companies from publishing their plays, often for years. Only 18 of Shakespeare's dramatic works were

By permission of the Governors of Dulwich Picture Gallery

Actor friends
The page from the First Folio of Shakespeare's plays (right) lists the main actors who appeared in them. The greatest among them was Richard Burbage (below), who was lionized by the public and much admired by his colleagues. Shakespeare remembered him in his will.

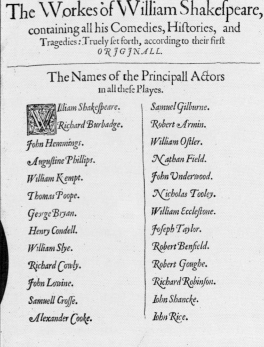

Fotomas Index

Prince of clowns
Will Kempe, shown left performing his famous dance from London to Norwich, was the star low comedian of Shakespeare's company.

Deadly enemy
(below) The plague closed down theatres during Shakespeare's career both in 1592-94 and 1603.

not because of the quality of his work, but because he was a shareholder in the Chamberlain's Men, later the King's Men, entitled to wear the royal livery and playing in two theatres.

The Globe, described by the Chorus in *Henry V* as 'this wooden O', was more or less circular, although this was not necessarily true of all Elizabethan theatres. The building was open to the sky, and performances were given, weather permitting, by the natural afternoon light. The stage projected right into the open area at the centre of the building, so that it was faced on three sides by the audience.

Fotomas Index

published during his lifetime, half a dozen of them probably without the owner's consent.

The owner of the text was not the dramatist but the company, which normally paid between £5 and £10 outright for a play. Authors did not make large sums of money. Most seem to have led a hand-to-mouth, bohemian existence, ending their lives in penury. Shakespeare was the exception –

At the back of the stage lay the changing room, known as the 'tiring house', which also served as scenery, representing a house, a castle or a hill. The actors made their entrances and exits through two doors in the tiring house, which also seems to have been equipped with windows and some sort of upper gallery serving as castle battlements, for example, and doubtless as a balcony in Romeo and Juliet's legendary love scene.

At the level of the stage, probably between the doors, an alcove provided an extra acting area where discoveries or concealments could be effected by drawing or closing curtains in front of it. In the stage itself, a trapdoor served as the gateway to the infernal regions: 'Ghost cries under the stage' reads one of the stage directions in Hamlet. Finally, a part of the acting area was covered by a star-decorated canopy, called the 'heavens', which protected the players from the elements.

In these conditions – acting in natural light, almost surrounded by the audience, with a fixed background and a relatively small number of 'props' – an Elizabethan performance cannot have been realistic in the modern sense. There were non-realistic acting conventions such as the soliloquy – a speech in which a character speaks alone to himself or addresses the audience, commenting on the action or revealing his thoughts. And all the female parts were played by boy apprentices; some of these youths must have been excellent actors, since Shakespeare went to the trouble of creating great (and difficult) female parts. He frequently devised plots, however, which involved women disguised as boys – a neat solution to problems of credibility.

A TASTE FOR SPECTACLE

Strenuous efforts were made to satisfy the Elizabethan taste for spectacle, surprise and horror – pigs' blood stored in a bladder and splashed about in the more gory scenes, splendid costumes, and the roar of a real cannon fired at some dramatic moment from the 'hut' at the top of the building. The best authorities advised actors to be 'natural', although standards of naturalness have changed so much over the centuries that it is hard to be sure what this means. In his famous speech to the players, Hamlet instructs them not to 'tear a passion to tatters' (over-act).

Since an Elizabethan actor must have relied heavily on the dialogue he spoke to create a sense of place and sustain the dramatic illusion, intelligent and intelligible delivery of his lines must have been one of his essential qualities. Elizabethans wrote of 'hearing' - not seeing - a performance. The emotional response achieved was evidently intense, and at the end of the proceedings, the tension was relaxed with a 'jig' involving slapstick clowning.

Elaborate staging can hardly have been possible for a small, busy company which put on a different play every afternoon for six days a week. In the course of a year the Chamberlain's Men performed some 40 plays, perhaps half of them new;

The Globe Theatre
The most famous of the Elizabethan theatres, the Globe (below) was the home of Shakespeare's company from 1599. In 1613 it was destroyed by fire (although it was during a performance, no-one was killed and 'only one man had his breeches set on fire'). It was rebuilt and reopened in 1614.

there was no such thing as a theatrical 'run', although popular plays would come round quickly and often.

The spectators usually paid a penny to enter the building, and were entitled to stand as 'groundlings' in the 'yard' around the stage. The better-off paid up to sixpence to go into the boxes next to the stage or the three galleries running round the walls. References to the groundlings in Elizabethan literature tend to be uncomplimentary; they were also known as 'stinkards', and Hamlet describes them as 'capable of nothing but inexplicable dumb shows and noise'. They were certainly capable of 'mewing' (cat-calling) bad

acting, but a penny was no small sum for a poor man to spend on entertainment, and the groundlings doubtless took the performance seriously. They may well have been less of a nuisance than the gallants who paid to sit on a stool right on the stage, where they smoked and gossiped and generally tried to attract attention away from the players to themselves.

The Elizabethan theatre matured with astonishing speed. Only a few years after the opening of the playhouse, great works of art were being written and new dramatic genres developed. Thomas Kyd introduced the revenge tragedy, popular for half a century. It contained elements which might seem faintly familiar: a noble young avenger, usually dressed in black, pausing frequently for set-piece soliloquies and real or feigned bouts of madness, is generally corrupted by his mission, before going down in a welter of blood in the final scene. *Hamlet* was no theatrical novelty.

INFLUENCE OF THE MASQUE

Chronicle plays also enjoyed an extraordinary boom. They frequently left history in a better state than the playwright found it, supplying interpretation of historical events in a way guaranteed to please the audience and the monarch. Shakespeare's history plays were the zenith of this play-form, too.

Command performance
Falstaff (above) is Shakespeare's greatest comic character. Shakespeare's first biographer, Nicholas Rowe (1709), said that Queen Elizabeth was so delighted with Falstaff in Henry IV *that she commanded Shakespeare to 'show him in love'. The result was* The Merry Wives of Windsor *(below).*

Shakespeare also emerged as master of romantic comedy, thus bringing to perfection all the genres which had gone before. He created in his last years great plays which defy classification. Written after the accession of James I in 1603, these late 'romances', in which dramatic realism gives place to fantasy and lyricism, show the growing influence of the masque.

The masque, a courtly entertainment involving music, dance and poetry, had seen one age of splendour during the reign of Henry VIII, but reached its ultimate glory under King James. The collaboration of playwright Ben Jonson and architect Inigo Jones resulted in entertainments of quite breathtaking extravagance, ingenuity and pomp. Massively complex stage machinery worked miraculous special effects; costumes and sets aspired to dream-like magnificence; and Jonson in particular brought a lyricism to the verse which leaves a worthwhile relic of an art form quite beyond replication these days. A modern audience might well find masques slow-moving, but there is no doubting the influence they had on playwrights of the time.

The 'Elizabethan' theatre lived on until 1642, when Puritans and Parliamentarians (who saw the playhouses as dens of iniquity) closed them down. Shakespeare's style of theatre, although certainly not his plays, had gone for good.

SAMUEL PEPYS

⟶ *1633-1703* ⟵

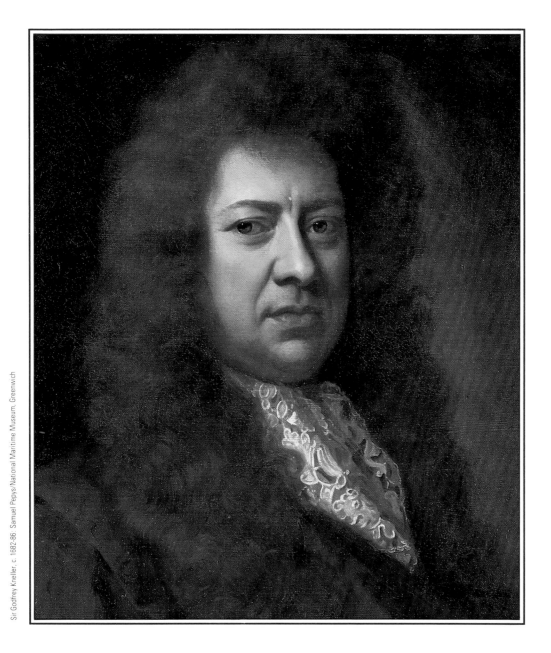

In his lifetime Samuel Pepys was respected as a dedicated administrator and as an enthusiastic supporter of science and the arts, but his greatest achievement did not become apparent until more than a century after his death, when his *Diary* was finally published. In addition to the wealth of information it offered to the social historian, this incomparable journal revealed the author as a warm, engaging man – diligent and learned, yet eager to enjoy all the pleasures that life had to offer.

Genius For Happiness

A lover of life, Pepys grabbed at all the pleasures that came his way, from the simple delights of playing his lute to the more sensuous appetites for fine food and beautiful women.

Fittingly, for one whose main claim to fame rests with his illuminating account of Restoration London, Samuel Pepys' origins lay close to the heart of the capital. He was born on 23 February 1633 in a room above the family shop in Salisbury Court, between Fleet Street and the Thames.

His father, John, was an impoverished tailor and his mother, Margaret Kite, had been a washerwoman. The family's fortunes were modest – largely because John Pepys was not a member of a guild and was therefore restricted in his trade – and Samuel grew up in dank, overcrowded conditions. He was born the fifth of 11 children but emerged as the eldest, since only four survived to maturity. The many thankful references which Pepys was to make in his *Diary* concerning his continuing good health are a telling reflection of the fragility of existence in 17th-century London.

Samuel's father was something of a poor relation within the Pepys clan. The family came from the Fenland region and, for generations, their ancestors had served as bailiffs to Crowland Abbey. Samuel was well aware of his distinguished origins and the *Diary* records his disappointment at being unable to find any mention of his forbears in Fuller's *Worthies* (the contemporary equivalent of *Who's Who*).

Samuel himself was sent to the grammar school at Huntingdon during the Civil War years. This was Cromwell country and it is hardly surprising that his upbringing was essentially Puritan in character. In 1649, he witnessed the execution of Charles I at Whitehall – the first of many that he was to attend during his lifetime.

By nature, Pepys was a lively and ebullient youth, with wide-ranging interests and a powerful capacity to enjoy himself. Wine, women and song, along with good food and fine clothes, were among his pleasures later in life. He was blessed with an excellent singing voice and played a number of musical instruments, once commenting playfully "Music and women I cannot but give way to, whatever my business is."

A HARDWORKING STUDENT

In his student days, however, he worked hard, first at St Paul's School in London and later at Magdalene College in Cambridge. There is one contemporary reference to him, though, which highlights the more self-indulgent side of his nature. In the College Order Book at Magdalene, he and a friend were severely reprimanded for being 'scandalously overserved with drink'.

Nevertheless, Pepys remained on good terms with both institutions. A friendly meeting with his

17th-century London
This view of the Thames (left) was commissioned by Pepys' contemporary and fellow-diarist John Evelyn. London at the time was developing at an inordinate rate as rural meadow land was transformed and absorbed into the city. "What will be the end of it, God knows!", Pepys exclaims in his Diary.

Royal execution

As a boy of 15 Pepys was at Whitehall to witness, approvingly, the execution of Charles I. However, in later years he changed position and became a committed Royalist.

Oliver Cromwell

Pepys grew to manhood during the Cromwellian Protectorate. Although he became a Royalist, he recognized Cromwell's stature, calling him a man of 'great courage'.

OLIVERIVS CROMWELL

Key Dates

1633 born in London

1642 outbreak of Civil War

1649 execution of Charles I

1650 Magdalene College, Cambridge

1655 marries Elizabeth St. Michel

1658 kidney stone removed

1660-69 *Diary*

1661 coronation of Charles II

1666 Great Fire

1683 visits Tangier

1685 coronation of James II

1703 dies in Clapham

on the subject, as he mastered its intricacies.

In 1654, aged 21, Pepys took his degree and returned to London. His activities during the next few years are largely obscure, although there was an important milestone in 1655, when he married Elizabeth St. Michel. Like his father before him, he had not made a conventionally advantageous match. Elizabeth was the daughter of a penniless French Huguenot and, by Pepys' standards, she was both ill-educated and hopelessly impractical. She was, however, very pretty.

The *Diary* provides a colourful account of their rollercoaster marriage, with Pepys frequently showing exasperation at her extravagance with clothes and her taste for reading lowbrow French romances. Elizabeth, for her part, was justifiably incensed at Pepys' habitual flirtations and dalliances with other women. For all that, the couple remained firmly in love. There are many occasions in the *Diary* when Pepys proudly noted how his wife's looks outshone those of the latest Court

old headmaster at St. Paul's is recorded in the *Diary*, while Magdalene College was ultimately to receive Pepys' most prized possession, his library. It was at Cambridge, too, that Pepys first took an interest in the shorthand methods which he was to employ in his *Diary*. Shelton's *Tachygraphy* – an early manual of shorthand – was available at the time, and Pepys eventually amassed a considerable collection of 32 books and pamphlets

A student at Cambridge

Pepys spent three years at Magdalene College, Cambridge (right). Apart from his academic studies, he learnt the method of shorthand he used in his Diary.

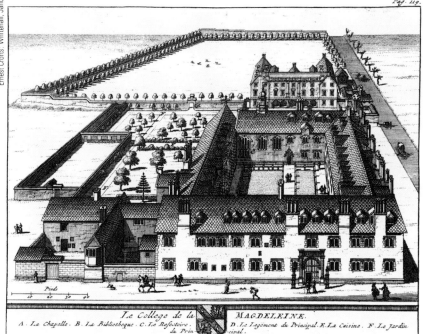

Le College de la MAGDELEINE.
A. La Chapelle. B. La Bibliotheque. C. Le Refectoire du Prin... D. Le Logement du Principal. E. La Cuisine. F. La Jardin...cipal.

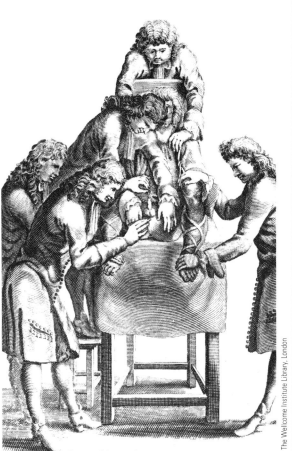

Laiouwe del et Sculp

'Cutting for the stone'
At 25 Pepys' pain from a kidney stone was so intense that he risked the dangers of an operation – without anaesthetic – to have it removed (above).

Crowned in glory
Pepys was at Westminster Abbey for the coronation of Charles II (right), a time when all the fountains in London ran with wine.

Bring out your dead
In 1666 the plague dominates Pepys' Diary. Estimates of the number of dead vary, but it was at least 70,000 – about one person in six.

favourite and it is significant that he never remarried after his wife's premature death in 1669.

The other major landmark in Pepys' early life occurred in 1658, when he underwent an operation for the removal of a kidney stone. This was very much a 'kill-or-cure' form of treatment in those days and Pepys was understandably aware of his good fortune in surviving it. The anniversary of the 'stone-cutting' day was usually mentioned in the *Diary* and, in the 1665 entry, Pepys informs us that he carried a hare's foot and took a daily dose of turpentine in the hope of staving off a recurrence of his malady.

AN INFLUENTIAL RELATIVE

Pepys' career, meanwhile, had begun to prosper. At around this time, he was appointed Clerk to George Downing, one of the four Tellers of the Exchequer. He owed this post to the influence of his first cousin, Edward Montagu, and he combined his new job with assorted administrative duties on behalf of his patron.

Pepys could hardly have been more fortunate in his connections. Although only eight years older than him, Montagu had already enjoyed a distinguished career as a Parliamentarian. He had fought at the Battle of Naseby (1645), had commanded a regiment of Oliver Cromwell's New Model Army and, in 1656, had been promoted to Joint Commander of the Fleet. However, he was essentially a moderate. He disapproved of Charles I's execution and, as the Commonwealth began to crumble following the death of Cromwell, he made secret overtures to the future Charles II, concerning his return from exile.

The results of these negotiations can be read in the opening pages of the *Diary*. Montagu read out

Carts full of dead to bury.

MICHIEL DE RUYTER

Born in 1607, Michiel de Ruyter is justifiably considered Holland's greatest admiral. He took on the British naval forces in the various Anglo-Dutch confrontations, distinguishing himself in the Four Days' Fight in June 1666 and again in his devastating raid on the Medway the following year, when he destroyed some of England's finest ships.

Return from exile
In May 1660 Pepys made a rare trip abroad to meet the exiled Charles II. Before sailing back with him from Scheveningen (left), he explored The Hague and Delft.

Anglo-Dutch wars
The 'Four Days' Fight' (above) was a catastrophe for the English. The Dutch admiral De Ruyter destroyed 20 English warships in this momentous battle, and after another disaster Pepys was called upon to defend the conduct of the Navy before the House of Commons.

Acts. Accordingly, in July 1660, he proudly moved with his wife into grander accommodation in Seething Lane, near the Tower of London.

Pepys brought to his new post the same diligence and attention to detail that had already impressed his patron. Although very much the junior member of the Board, he worked long hours and was willing to learn. In addition, he maintained his integrity in an age when corruption and bribery were commonplace. For, though he did not refuse some of the small 'presents' that came his way, it often astonished him to think of the temptations that were open to a man in his position. "Good God! To see what a man might do, were I a knave!" he remarked, after negotiating a lucrative contract for the purchase of masts.

AFTERNOONS OF PLEASURE

Pepys continued to make sporadic references to his work in the *Diary* but, overall, his journal is more illuminating for the insights it gives us into the author's own character and for its portrayal of the entertainments that were available to Londoners in the early years of the Restoration.

Pepys was a methodical, hard-working man, often rising soon after dawn to go to work and occasionally remaining at the office in the evening. The afternoons, however, were usually devoted to pleasure and it was at this time that he made his frequent theatre visits. Pepys made great efforts to limit this 'extravagance', even going to the extent of paying self-imposed penalties (a crown in the church poorbox). The resulting economies could prove an embarrassment, however, and on one occasion he was mortified to find himself observed by four of the office clerks while he was sitting in the cheap seats.

Pepys' frugality was a legacy, no doubt, of his Puritan upbringing and his early financial struggles. In other respects, however, he displayed a capacity for enjoyment that was more in tune with the times. The *Diary* is peppered with references to his love of good wine and food, his vanity about clothes – he was, after all, the son of a tailor – and his appreciation of the beauty of the king's mistresses or of the latest fashionable actress.

the Declaration of Breda – Charles' proposals for forming a new government – to the officers of the Fleet and Pepys was among the party which sailed to The Hague, in May 1660, to escort the new king home. Montagu was rewarded for his services with the Order of the Garter and the title of Earl of Sandwich, and he vowed to reward his cousin. 'We will rise together', he promised.

Montagu was as good as his word. Amid the welter of changes which accompanied the restoration of the monarchy, the old Navy Board was re-established and, through his cousin's influence, Pepys was able to secure the post of Clerk of the

Pepys derived equal enjoyment from spectacles of any kind. He described himself quaintly as "with child to see any strange thing" and he despaired of the insularity of his fellow-countrymen. His own voracious curiosity took him to such diverse events as cock-fights and boxing matches, in addition to the staple entertainments of plays and public executions.

UNEXPECTED COURAGE

The same spirit of enquiry also fuelled Pepys' interest in the early activities of the Royal Society, the leading scientific institution. He was elected a member in 1665, attended many of the lectures at Gresham College and ultimately, in 1684, was created President of the Society. Even so, his attitude on some occasions appears to have been a little credulous, notably in his talk with the antiquary Elias Ashmole, "wherein he did assure me that frogs and many insects do often fall from the sky, ready formed".

We are fortunate that the brief span of the *Diary* also encompassed three major historical events. In two of these – the Great Plague and the Fire of London – Pepys was directly involved. During the former, he showed an unexpected courage that contrasts sharply with his timidity at other times, while his account of the Fire reveals his journalist's eye, in capturing the bustle and the panic of the situation. Where another writer like John Evelyn used solemn, classical allusions to convey the tragedy of the event, Pepys' description is full of vivid anecdotes. We learn that the fashion for periwigs declined, as people feared that the hair

from which they were made had been cut from the bodies of plague victims; and we read of how Pepys and his colleagues dug pits during the Fire, to conserve their wine and Parmesan cheese.

The third disaster also touched Pepys deeply, although he was not involved at first hand. This concerned the series of naval disasters inflicted by the Dutch, which culminated, in June 1667, in Admiral de Ruyter's forces sailing up the Medway and destroying the English fleet.

The continuing naval crisis extended beyond the scope of the *Diary*. In 1667, 1668 and 1670,

Aristocratic links
Throughout the Diary *Pepys makes reference to the Duke of York and his wife Anne Hyde (above). He had particular respect for the Duke (the future James II) who, as High Admiral of England, was his superior while Pepys served as Secretary of the Navy.*

Tragedy at sea
A new war with the Dutch had disastrous repercussions both publicly and privately for Pepys. England was sucked into this third Anglo-Dutch confrontation by the Treaty of Dover, in which Charles II schemed with his cousin, Louis XIV of France, to invade the Netherlands and carve up the country between them, leaving only a small part as nominally independent. However, they misjudged the Dutch, who in spite of their smaller navy were more than a match for the British. Early on in the two-year war, Pepys' cousin, friend and benefactor, Montagu, the Earl of Sandwich, was blown up in the disastrous Battle of Sole Bay in 1672 (left).

A trip to Tangier
As secretary to Lord Dartmouth, Pepys sailed to Tangier (above) in 1683 to arrange the evacuation of this costly and difficult-to-defend British colony, which had been acquired in 1661 as part of Catherine of Braganza's Portuguese dowry to Charles II.

honours were heaped upon him, including being installed as the Master of Trinity House (an association of mariners) in 1676.

The remarkable progress of Pepys' career was rudely interrupted in 1679, however, when he was accused of selling naval secrets to the French. Although this bogus charge was eventually dropped, he spent six weeks in the Tower and was obliged to resign from his Admiralty post. The real problem, here, came from the growing backlash against Catholicism. Pepys had been suspected of Papist sympathies for some years and his long association with James, Duke of York (the future James II), marked him out as an enemy of the Protestant faction. In the religious sense, at least, these claims were quite unjustified. The frequent references in the *Diary* to "drowsy sermons" clearly show that Pepys was no zealot.

A HAPPY RETIREMENT

In the mid 1680s Pepys experienced a brief return to power. He was reinstated to the Admiralty office in 1684 and in 1685 helped carry the royal canopy during the coronation of James II. However, this interlude was terminated by the Glorious Revolution of 1688 which placed the Protestant William of Orange on the English throne. In the following year, aged 56, Pepys retired from public life.

In his later years, Pepys spent much time entertaining his friends from the Royal Society at his home in Buckingham Street, Westminster and devoted many hours to expanding and cataloguing his superb collection of books.

Pepys' closest friends during this final period were his housekeeper, Mary Skynner, and his former clerk, William Hewer, who later became Governor of the East India Company. It was to Hewer's Clapham home that Pepys retired, when his health began to fail, and it was there that he died some months later, on 26 May 1703.

On the day of his death, his fellow-diarist John Evelyn recorded an elegant tribute, describing him as 'a very worthy, industrious and curious person . . . hospitable, generous, learned in many things . . . a very great cherisher of learned men.'

Pepys was called upon by Parliament to defend the Navy's administration of its resources and, on each occasion, he acquitted himself nobly. However, after the secret Treaty of Dover (1670), in which Charles II and Louis XIV connived at the partition of Dutch territories, a third Anglo-Dutch War was inevitable. This broke out in 1672 and, in one of the opening confrontations, Pepys' loyal cousin Montagu lost his life.

Montagu's death was the culmination of a wretched period in Pepys' private life. In 1669, he abandoned his *Diary* out of fear (groundless, as it transpired) that he would lose his sight and, in the same year, his young wife died of fever after a brief trip to Paris and Brussels. Pepys threw himself ever more energetically into his work and the next few years saw him reach the pinnacle of his career.

In 1673, he was appointed Secretary to the Admiralty – a major post, enabling him to carry through the reforms that were so long overdue. In the same year, he was elected MP for Castle Rising and he retained a seat in Parliament – though mostly as MP for Harwich – until 1689. Further

William Hewer
In 1660, a 17-year-old youth, Will Hewer (above), joined Pepys' household as part-time clerk, and it was to his house, 41 years later, that Pepys retired to spend his remaining years with his friend.

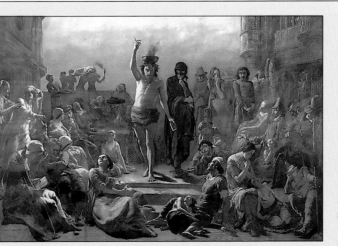

Fact or Fiction

SOLOMON 'EAGLE'

On 29 July 1667 Pepys saw a half-naked man running through Westminster Hall with a bowl of fire on his head, urging people to repent. This was Solomon Eccles (1618-83), an eccentric Quaker who was notorious for his dramatic demonstrations. During the plague years he was a common sight in the streets of London, and in 1722 Defoe described him as 'the famous Solomon Eagle (sic) . . . not infected at all but in his head'.

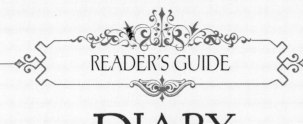

DIARY

Pepys' *Diary* is the most famous book of its type ever written – a matchless source of gossip and information, as well as a touching, humorous picture of its warm-hearted author.

Pepys' famous *Diary*, written between 1 January 1660 and 31 May 1669, is one of the most fascinating personal documents ever published. When it first appeared in abridged form in 1825, the *Diary* caused an immediate sensation and the revelations it contains have continued to amuse and delight countless readers ever since. That the diary of a relatively unknown 17th-century civil servant should excite such interest and admiration might seem odd. But on opening the first page the reader is at once captivated by the personal panorama of love, marriage, court intrigue, gossip, scandal, political skulduggery, work, play, eating, drinking, getting up and going to bed. And apart from its intensely human interest, the *Diary* provides a unique portrait of London in one of its most exciting periods – the decade that witnessed the Restoration, the Plague and the Great Fire.

OUTLINE OF EVENTS

Pepys begins his *Diary* on 1 January 1660. England is in political turmoil. For over ten years, since the execution of King Charles I in 1649, the country has been a republic, ruled first by Oliver Cromwell, then – after his death in 1658 – by his son Richard, deposed in 1659. Parliament has been dissolved and the Army holds power. As Pepys reveals, in the early months of 1660 there is popular support and political intrigue for the restoration of King Charles II, who is living in exile in Holland. When elections are held in March 1660 for a new Parliament, an overwhelming number of Royalist members are returned. Events move swiftly, and in April Parliament invites Charles to return.

When ships are despatched to bring the exiled King home, the 27-year-old Pepys is sent as secretary and treasurer to the Fleet. He spends two weeks in Holland, and on 17 May is introduced to the King ("a very sober man"), as well as to Charles' brother James, Duke of York.

An eye for beauty
Frances Stewart (left), later Duchess of Richmond, is one of many beauties extolled in the Diary. *"With her sweet eye, little Roman nose, and excellent* taille *[figure]", she was "the greatest beauty I ever saw".*

A joyous welcome
(above) Charles II's return from exile was met with euphoria. "The shouting and joy expressed by all is past imagination", wrote Pepys of the King's arrival at Dover. Londoners were equally ecstatic.

40

records the effects of his own private celebrations: "no sooner a-bed . . . but my head began to turn, and I to vomit, and if ever I was foxed, it was now."

With the monarchy firmly re-established, Pepys settles down to his work, from which he derives great pleasure, and records his day-to-day experiences, observations and impressions. After the euphoria of the Restoration, doubts grow about those who surround the King. "At court", Pepys writes on 31 August 1661, "things are in very ill condition, there being so much . . . drinking, swearing, and loose amours, that I know not what will be the end of it but confusion."

A NOBLE DINNER

On the personal and domestic level, Pepys records meeting his many friends and entertaining them to dinner. "January 13th, 1663. My poor wife rose by five o'clock in the morning . . . and went to market and bought fowls and many other things for dinner, with which I was highly pleased . . . By and by comes Dr Clerke, and his lady, his sister, and a she-cousin, and Mr Pierce and his wife, which was all my guests. I had for them, after

On 23 May Pepys sets sail for England aboard the *London* with the King. For his loyal services he is promoted to Clerk of the Acts to the Navy Board.

The bloodbath that many feared would accompany the Restoration does not happen. Only those personally responsible for the execution of Charles I are punished. "I went to Charing Cross to see Major-General Harrison hanged, drawn, and quartered", writes Pepys on 13 October 1660, "he looking as cheerful as any man could do in that condition. He

The Great Fire
(above) Pepys' description is the most vivid we have of the horror that engulfed London.

In the tavern
(right) Eating and drinking gave Pepys great pleasure. The Diary has many accounts of culinary delights.

The sound of music
(left) Pepys loved music passionately, both to listen to and to perform.

was presently cut down, and his head and heart shown to the people, at which there was great shouts of joy."

On Coronation Day, 23 April 1661, Pepys records, "About four I rose and got to the Abbey . . . where with a great deal of patience I sat . . . till eleven before the King came in." Characteristically he notes that as the King leaves Westminster Abbey, "it fell a-raining and thundering and lightening as I have not seen it do for some years." Equally characteristically he

oysters . . . a hash of rabbits and lamb, and a rare chine of beef. Next, a great dish of roasted fowl . . . and a tart and then fruit and cheese. My dinner was noble, and enough."

Pepys, however, is not often so pleased with his "poor wife". The entry for 6 January 1663 is typical: "somewhat vexed at my wife's neglect in leaving of her scarf, waistcoat, and night-dressings in the coach to-day", although his essential honesty forces him to "confess she did give them to me to look after".

So the years pass in working, feasting, drinking, buying clothes, noting the latest fashion for periwigs, quarrelling with his wife, taking stock of his wealth and his wine-cellar, witnessing hangings, attending cock-fights, until the tragic year 1665. The plague strikes, and on 26 July Pepys notes: "Sad news of death of so many in the parish of the plague; forty last night; the bell always going." By 12 August he reports disconsolately: "The people die so, that now it seems they are fain to carry the dead to be buried by daylight, the nights not sufficing to do it in."

'SO MANY POOR SICK PEOPLE'

The number of plague deaths continues to mount throughout the next two months. "How empty the streets are, and melancholy, so many poor sick people in the streets full of sores", he observes on 16 October, "and so many sad stories overheard as I walk, everybody talking of this dead, and that man sick, and so many in this place, and so many in that." Not until November does the plague abate.

Not even the plague can dampen his spirits for long, however. "December

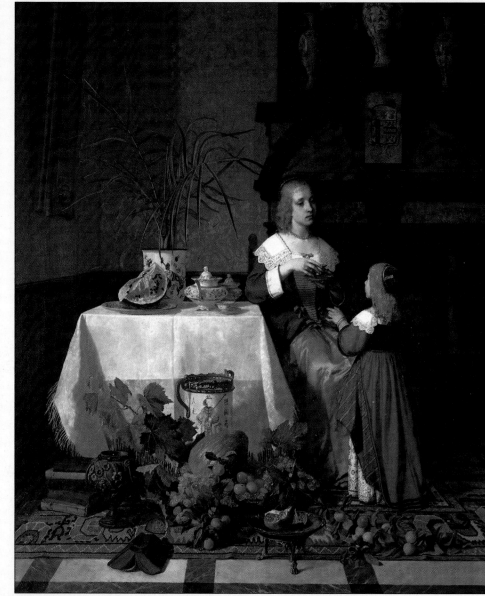

Noter and Koller: Tea Time: Christie's, London/Bridgeman Art Library

Strolling in the park
(below) St James's park, here shown looking towards Whitehall, was a popular haunt. Pepys often mentions the people he saw there, including the King and his mistresses.

Domestic fashions
Pepys' Diary, with its wealth of detail about everyday life, is the richest source we have for 17th-century social history. He describes, for example, the novelty of tea drinking (right).

Jan Wyck: Horseguards Parade (detail)/Oscar and Peter Johnson Ltd, London/Bridgeman Art Library

6th. To Mrs Pierce's . . . Here the best company for music I ever was in, in my life, and wish I could live and die in it, both for music and the face of Mrs Pierce, and my wife, and Knipp, who is pretty enough." The next year brings fresh trials and tribulations. "September 2nd, 1666. Jane [the maid] called us up about three in the morning, to tell us of a great fire in the City." The "great fire" was to destroy a third of London in four days. Pepys' lengthy eye-witness account captures the full devastation of the event.

The following year, 1667, Pepys faces the loss of personal prestige when the Dutch fleet under Admiral de Ruyter sails up the River Medway in June, captures the Navy's flagship the *Royal Charles* and destroys three other first-rate warships. On 21 June he notes with dismay, "the Court is as mad as ever . . . the night the Dutch burned our ships the King did sup with my Lady Castlemaine, at the Duchess of Monmouth's, and there were all mad in the hunting of a poor moth."

After the invasion scare, Pepys has to defend his office, and on 5 March 1668 addresses the House of Commons. He rises brilliantly to the occasion: "All my fellow-officers and all the world that was within hearing, did congratulate me, and cry up my speech as the best thing they ever heard." Pepys is understandably delighted by the accolades he receives. The next day he relates: "going to the parke, and by and by overtaking the King, the King and Duke of York came to me both, and he said, 'Mr Pepys, I am very glad of your success yesterday;' and fell to talk of my well speaking . . ."

Thus exonerated, Pepys settles down once more to hard work and hard play. He visits Epsom Downs, chronicles the fall of Lord Chancellor Clarendon, watches a game of tennis, agonizes over some lost gold buried during the invasion scare, notes the vanity of the age and on 31 May 1669 makes his last entry. He feared for his eyesight and sadly concludes: "And thus ends all that I doubt I shall ever be able to do with my own eyes in the keeping of my Journal."

A SOCIAL DOCUMENT

The setting of the *Diary* is London. Apart from a few brief excursions further afield – to Holland, Cambridge, Huntingdon and Epsom – Pepys spent most of his time in the capital, so the *Diary* is essentially a record of London life in the 1660s. As a source of social history, it is unique for its detail about people and manners. From Pepys we learn about eating and drinking

Prince Rupert
(above) One of Charles II's admirals, Rupert came into conflict with Pepys over naval matters. However, Pepys admired his courage.

Beauty patches
In his Diary *entry for 12 November 1660 Pepys writes: "My wife seemed very pretty to-day, it being the first time I had given her leave to wear a black patch." The fashion attracted much mockery (right).*

habits, what amused people, what they wore and how they behaved.

Pepys moved from the public to the private domain easily and naturally and his writing reflects this. Little escapes his notice. When he hears the cry of the bellman under his window as he writes his entry for 16 January 1660, he records it: "Past one of the clock, and a cold, frosty, windy morning." Above all the *Diary* is a personal record, the chronicle of a man who, from the time he gets up in the morning and takes his "morning draught" to the time he goes to bed, loved life.

Until 1818 the six leather-bound volumes of the *Diary* lay undisturbed in one of the twelve glass-fronted bookcases that Pepys bequeathed to his old college –

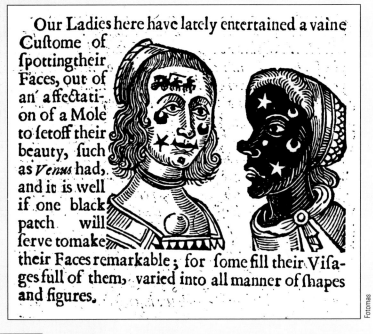

Our Ladies here have lately entertained a vaine Custome of spotting their Faces, out of an affectation of a Mole to setoff their beauty, such as *Venus* had, and it is well if one black patch will serve tomake their Faces remarkable; for some fill their Visages full of them, varied into all manner of shapes and figures.

| In the Background |

REBUILDING LONDON

Although the Great Fire of 1666 is the most famous disaster in London's history, it was a calamity with compensations. The loss of life was small, and the destruction of the tightly packed wooden buildings that had allowed the fire to spread so rapidly gave England's most famous architect, Sir Christopher Wren (left), the opportunity to plan the grandiose rebuilding of the city. His town-planning scheme was too ambitious to be completed, but he designed more than 50 new churches for London, including his masterpiece St Paul's Cathedral (its dome is shown behind him in the portrait).

Magdalene – at Cambridge. In that year, however, the diary of Pepys' friend John Evelyn was published, and this inspired the Master of Magdalene College to commission an undergraduate called John Smith to transcribe Pepys' shorthand. Apart from omitting certain 'objectionable' passages, Smith transcribed the entire text, and an abridged edition of the *Diary* was published in 1825.

Many other editions have followed, but the first complete text (including explicit erotic passages omitted from all earlier editions) did not appear until 1970-76, when a definitive nine-volume edition was published. An index and a companion volume of notes appeared later. It has been hailed as one of the greatest works of literary scholarship of the 20th century, and the dedication and skill of the editors would surely have won the admiration of the hardworking Pepys himself.

CHARACTERS IN FOCUS

Pepys' *Diary* mentions hundreds of people: the King and members of his court; family, friends and colleagues; and other characters of all kinds whom the author meets in the course of his varied and busy life. Many of these people make only brief appearances in the *Diary* – including the sometimes nameless women with whom Pepys pursues his 'amours' – but others play leading roles, helping to shape the author's life.

WHO'S WHO

Samuel Pepys The writer of the *Diary*, an industrious naval administrator and *bon vivant*.

Charles II King of England, who at the beginning of the *Diary* returns in triumph from exile.

Catherine of Braganza Daughter of the King of Portugal, she is Charles II's barren and much-abused Queen.

Sir Edward Montagu, Earl of Sandwich Pepys' cousin and patron, distinguished as a soldier, a naval commander and a statesman.

Edward Hyde, Earl of Clarendon Charles II's Lord Chancellor, in effect head of the government.

Elizabeth Pepys Pepys' wife, who delights and exasperates her husband.

Paulina (Pall) Pepys Pepys' sister, for whom he endeavours to find a husband, "for she grows old and ugly".

Will Hewer Pepys' clerk in the Naval Office and his lifelong friend.

Sir William Penn Pepys' superior in the Naval Office – much disliked by him and abused in the *Diary*.

Lady Castlemaine Charles II's most enduring mistress, the mother of five of his children.

Nell Gwyn A leading comic actress and Charles' most famous mistress; illegitimate, illiterate and warm-hearted, she is much loved by the populace.

The beautiful Lady Castlemaine (right), the wife of a distinguished diplomat and scholar, became Charles II's regular mistress soon after he returned to England. But she is only one of many royal concubines and in July 1663 "she looked mighty out of humour . . . very melancholy", plagued by jealousy towards the 16-year-old Mrs Stewart.

"A very sober man" is Pepys' first impression of King Charles II (below), but he later revises this view. Although a loyal subject, Pepys is shocked by the frivolity of Court life. "God help the King while no better counsels are given, and what is given no better taken." Pepys goes on to chronicle Charles' numerous amours but also recognizes his stabilizing effects on the nation.

Laroon: Charles II as President of the Royal Society/Christ's Hospital/E. T. Archive

"A most able and ready man", **Edward Hyde,** the Earl of Clarendon (right) was Lord Chancellor of England. Pepys personally incurred the displeasure of this unpopular statesman by ordering, in the course of his work, "the trees in Clarendon Park marked and cut down". Despite having been the King's advisor in exile, Clarendon was made a scapegoat for all catastrophes. The sale of Dunkirk, the Dutch war, even the Plague and the Great Fire contributed to his mounting unpopularity. In 1667 he was stripped of his seal of office and, later, impeached for high treason. Pepys charts the downfall in his *Diary*.

"We will rise together . . . and I will do you all the good jobs I can", promised Pepys' cousin, mentor and patron Edward Montagu (below), and he secured for Pepys the post of secretary and treasurer to the Fleet. Montagu was made Earl of Sandwich and General-at-Sea as rewards for his major role in the King's Restoration.

Elizabeth Pepys (right) is 19 years old and has been married to Pepys for four years when the *Diary* opens. Her untidiness and carelessness vex her husband and he constantly upbraids her for her extravagance. "My wife being dressed this day in fair hair did make me so mad that I spoke not one word to her, though I was ready to burst with anger." Such entries are common. Yet she has much more to put up with. Frequently left alone but for the company of Pepys' unpleasant father, she has to forgive her husband's meannesses and infidelities. He is proud of her beauty, at least, owning her to be "extraordinary fine" and "handsome". For all their quarrelling, they were an affectionate couple and Pepys mourned her early death deeply.

A PANORAMIC VIEW

Pepys' private record of everyday 17th-century life has achieved fame as a work of literature, although written without literary pretensions, with no audience in mind – except perhaps posterity.

It is a remarkable fact that Samuel Pepys, who concealed so little in his *Diary*, never tells us why he started to write it, or what kind of satisfaction he got from doing so. Since his daily record begins on 1 January 1660, the equivalent of a New Year resolution may have played some part in setting him to work on it. And with the Cromwellian republic in disarray and momentous changes imminent, he was almost certainly moved to set down his impressions of historic events as they occurred. But even if these formed the immediate inspiration for his *Diary*, there must also have been more enduring impulses that kept Pepys writing away for nine years, creating an account that covers every day of his life except for one short period in 1668, when he went on holiday and never wrote up the notes he kept.

A CANDID APPRAISAL

In the 17th century it was common to keep diaries, but not to publish them, so that each diarist, including Pepys, effectively had to invent his or her own version of the genre. Many were essentially scrupulous self-examinations of the kind encouraged by Puritanism and also found in published autobiographies, such as John Bunyan's *Grace Abounding to the Chief of Sinners*. Pepys may have been influenced by this outlook, although his self-examinations were concerned with his worldly rather than his spiritual condition. Despite being a regular churchgoer, he tackled everyday life in an emphatically secular frame of mind. Other contemporary diarists and autobiographers noted down their worldly successes, or their travels, or the great events they lived through (though not all three); and a few women writers give us glimpses of their personal relationships and intimate emotions. But there is no one to match the variety, fullness and candour of Pepys.

Pepys is interested in himself and his own doings, and is exact or vain enough to record trivial matters (what he wore, the arrival of a barrel of oysters, the quality of the dinner he gave his friends, reading "a mighty lewd book") which have

Words and music
One-and-a-quarter million words were transcribed from Pepys' six volumes (above right) of neat and revised 'short-writing' (above) – but not until a century after their author's death. They grant insight into a colourful character – a man ravished by music and literature (right), yet with an earthy, far-from-elevated preoccupation with the delights of the other senses, too.

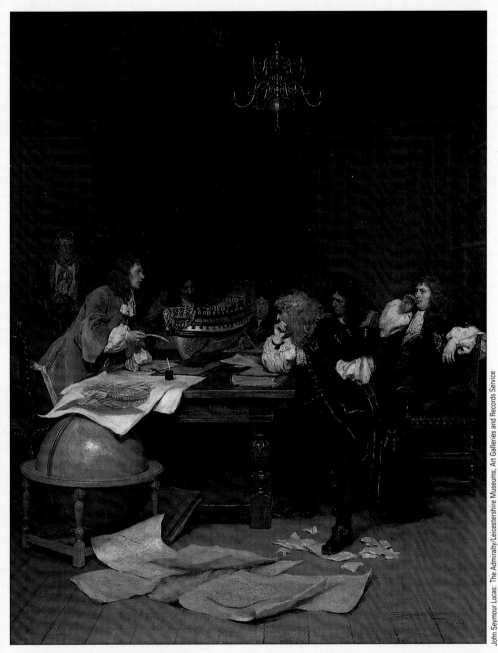

Pepys is unusual in combining this immense zest with the supposedly pedestrian qualities of an able administrator: a compulsion to organize, classify and record everything that came to hand. This must have been a major motive for keeping the *Diary*, which is in fact only one element in Pepys' self-administration. He also kept a meticulous official business journal (called the 'Navy White-Book'), a memorandum book, a letter book, accounts, a petty cash book, and even separate records of vows he had made and stories he had heard. In part, at least, we owe the wide-ranging delights of the *Diary* to the fact that Pepys was an extreme case of the 'civil service mentality'. Certainly he loved his job in the Navy Office, and the only book he published in his lifetime – *Memoires Relating to the State of the Royal Navy* (1690) – was a commentary on it.

OPEN SECRETS

Most of the one-and-a-quarter-million words in the *Diary* were written in shorthand, although Pepys spelled out many proper names, such as those of people, places and books. Shorthand has a long history (it was practised by the ancient Greeks), but it had been known in England only from Elizabethan times. It was looked on as an arcane branch of learning rather than merely a stenographic device, so it is hardly surprising that Pepys, a man of scientific curiosity, should have studied Thomas Shelton's *Tutor to Tachygraphy, or Short-writing* while an undergraduate.

Shelton's system was well-known (Sir Isaac Newton also used it), so it did not function as a cypher, guaranteed to baffle

entertained posterity as much as his more weighty occupations. Yet he is also intensely involved in the world about him as both a participant and an eager observer. And as a public servant he is deeply affected by current affairs, putting down what he knows and (for he is not at the very heart of power) such uncertain news as gossip and rumours bring.

He had a remarkably wide range of interests, and his love of the good things in life shines from the pages of his *Diary*. Food, drink, music, the theatre and books were all things that gave him immense pleasure, and he could never resist a pretty face. Although many shadows – great and small – passed over his life (the Plague, the Fire of London, his bickering with his wife), he was never downcast for long, and always bounced back to his normal high spirits: he has been aptly described as having a 'genius for happiness'.

The civil servant
Pepys' meticulous nature and love of paperwork were well-suited to the Navy Office (above). In this Victorian reconstruction, Pepys is the ruddy-faced man looking out in the centre.

Writing at leisure
Pepys' account of the Great Fire (right) is an instance of the way he drew on notes taken at the time of an event in order to write them up in detail some time later.

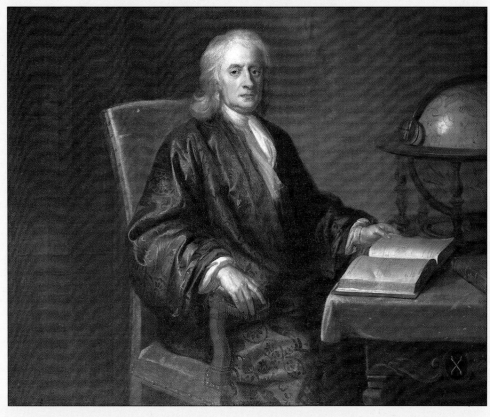

The Writer at Work

all outsiders. Indeed, Pepys employed shorthand for all sorts of ordinary business, simply because it was quick and labour-saving. Nevertheless it did afford a measure of privacy within Pepys' immediate circle, including his wife. He eventually thought it necessary to add a layer of further concealment by recording his sexual activities in a rough-and-ready mixture of Spanish, French, Dutch and several other languages. The importance of this secrecy is indicated in the final diary entry of 31 May 1669. Anticipating blindness, Pepys wrote that any future

Naval engagements
Although Pepys spent most of his time in London, his job took him to places such as Dover (below). He usually rose very early and often worked late, but still found time for his voluminous Diary.

Man of science
As President of the Royal Society, Pepys was responsible for authorizing the publication of the work of Sir Isaac Newton (right). Pepys' interest in science was wide-ranging, and he was intrigued by scientific aspects of music.

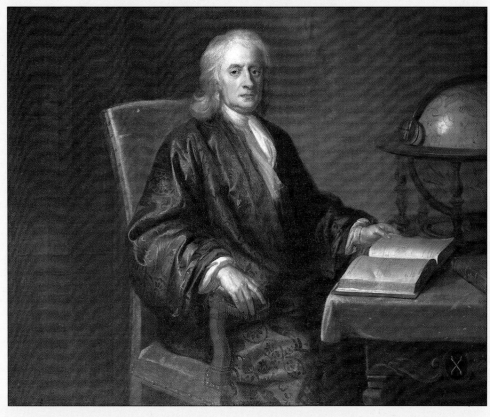
National Portrait Gallery, London

Jacob Knyff. Charles II on board a two-decker man-o'-war off Dover/Private Collection/Bridgeman Art Library

48

diary would have to be "kept by my people in longhand"; he "must therefore be contented to set down no more than is fit for them and all the world to know".

CAREFUL CORRECTION

At first sight it seems curious that an extremely busy man such as Pepys should have written a diary – intended for his eyes alone – in eloquent prose rather than in the form of notes and jottings. The entries were originally believed to represent spontaneous outpourings written without any significant preliminaries. But modern studies of the text suggest that Pepys was in reality a conscious literary artist who made extensive use of rough notes, office memoranda and other source material, which he drew together in accounts covering several days at a time. And we know that one of the celebrated set pieces of the *Diary*, his description of the Great Fire of London, was added some three months after the event.

Some entries, in terse note-form, were clearly written in haste, but the text generally conveys the opposite impression. In fact, the extreme neatness of the short-

Fellow diarist
John Evelyn (right) had much in common with Pepys. Both, in turn, were presidents of the Royal Society and both kept diaries – although Evelyn's has none of Pepys' characteristic verve and immediacy. Pepys was Evelyn's "particular friend for near forty years". At Pepys' death he called him "a very worthy, industrious and curious person, none in England exceeding him in knowledge of the navy . . . universally beloved, hospitable, generous, learned in many things, skilled in music, a very great cherisher of learned men".

Pepys in print
The volume at left is the only book Pepys published in his lifetime. The title page quotation from the Roman author Cicero – 'What sweeter than scholarly leisure?' – reflects the pleasures Pepys found in his retirement, reading, researching and writing.

Fotomas

'Journal', which seems like an extra signal to posterity that the contents ought to be examined. So perhaps Pepys did, after all, write with readers in mind – the readers of the future, whom he probably visualized as scholarly researchers into either history or human nature.

UNREAD TREASURES

Remarkably, although Shelton's shorthand remained quite well known, Pepys' diaries lay unread, or at least unremarked, throughout the 18th century. The first passage that was seen by the public ran "I did send for a cup of tea (a China drink) of which I never had drunk before". This was taken from the entry for 25 September 1660 and quoted in a book on European commerce with India published in 1812. The first published edition of the diary (1825) contained little more than a quarter of the text, but it was an instant success. It certainly encouraged Sir Walter Scott to begin a journal of his own in the same year. New editions followed in rapid succession, and within a few years Pepys' *Diary*, utterly unknown for so long, had become one of the great popular classics of the language.

hand – and the nature of some of Pepys' errors – make it highly likely that he habitually made a first draft before setting down an entry (effectively a fair copy) in the *Diary*. On the other hand, although at first carefully corrected (the number of emendations has been estimated at 4,000), the text was not subsequently revised. Oddly enough, given his meticulousness, Pepys never filled in the blanks he left for names which had slipped his memory.

The care Pepys took in writing his *Diary*

was matched by the care he took to preserve it. During crises such as the Great Fire and the Dutch raid down the Medway, he sent these 'Journalls which I value much' out of the danger zone and into the safe-keeping of friends. From the beginning they were protected by sturdy bindings, and later they were included in the choice library that Pepys bequeathed to Magdalene College, Cambridge, 'for the benefit of posterity'. By this time each of the six diary volumes was clearly labelled

49

PEPYS' LIBRARY

Pepys devoted much of his leisure time to assembling a choice collection of books, manuscripts and engravings. His library was his pride and joy, and he took great care over its arrangement and cataloguing – indeed he is regarded as a pioneer of library science (his own handwritten catalogues are preserved with his books and are still used as a guide to them). Pepys bequeathed his cherished library to his devoted nephew John Jackson on the understanding that subsequently it would pass to Magdalene College, Cambridge. Still housed in their purpose-built cases, Pepys' books now form one of the cultural gems of the city. Many famous libraries are much larger than Pepys', but few give such a clear picture of the taste and discrimination of their founders.

LITERARY TREASURE HOUSE. Pepys had great affection for his old college at Cambridge – Magdalene – so it is fitting that his library should find its final home there. The building in which it is housed (below) was begun in the 1670s and Pepys – appropriately – was one of the subscribers towards its cost. The glass-fronted bookcases are contained in a single room (right) on the main wall of which hangs a portrait of Pepys. His love of order is revealed in the meticulous arrangement of his treasures – on most shelves there is a row of small books in front of a row of much bigger volumes. Pepys was more interested in quality than quantity and set himself a limit of 3000 volumes – a figure he knew could just be accommodated in his bookcases. Since his bequest nothing has been added to the library, which – next to the *Diary* – is his greatest memorial.

PEPYS' MANUSCRIPTS. The library contains not only printed books, but also many fascinating manuscripts, including the shorthand volumes of the *Diary*. As befitted a great music lover, Pepys collected much material relating to his favourite art. He also owned several medieval illuminated manuscripts, including the one showing various birds and beasts – real and imaginary – above left. The pelican is shown piercing its breast so it can feed its young with its blood – a symbol of Christ's sacrifice on the cross. Nearer to Pepys' main interests is the manuscript illumination of a Tudor ship (left). Given to Pepys by Charles II, it comes from a volume depicting Henry VIII's navy. Pepys planned to write a history of the navy and collected a great deal of research material for it, but it was never completed.

Cpagina prima.

Cntroductorium lingue latine.

BIBLIOGRAPHICAL RARITIES. Pepys' library contains many rare and beautiful books including the Latin grammar (above) published by Wynkyn de Worde (William Caxton's successor) in 1495. Schoolbooks such as this were often used until they were worn out or thrown away when they became obsolete, and the Pepys copy is the only one of this edition known to have survived.

Pepys was extremely exacting about the quality of his books, and on 2 February 1668 he wrote in his *Diary*: "All the morning setting my books in order in my presses [cases] . . . I am fain to lay by several books to make room for better, being resolved to keep no more than just my presses will contain." He devoted much of his retirement to organising his library.

BEAUTIFUL BINDINGS. In Pepys' day new books were often sold without a permanent cover so that the book buyer could have them bound to his own requirements – often to match other volumes in his collection. Pepys cared as much about the exterior of his books as he did about the contents (as can be seen from the superb binding left). In his search for fine books he was assisted by his faithful nephew John Jackson, who in 1699 went to Italy and Spain to buy books and prints on behalf of his uncle.

Restoration Drama

"How easily my mind do revert to its former practice of loving plays." Pepys rejoiced when the theatres, closed for 18 years, opened their doors to a new, ebullient kind of drama.

In his *Diary*, Pepys records many changes in the English way of life that occurred after the restoration of the monarchy in 1660. In particular, the reappearance of plays on the London stage, after an absence of 18 years, met with his wholehearted approval. He was an ardent theatregoer and wrote a play himself in his student days.

The theatres were officially closed by the Puritans in 1642. During the years that followed, however, the ban was persistently and variously flouted. Halls and inns were used as makeshift stages for the performance of 'drolls' – comic revues, adapted from existing plays. Thus, the more farcical elements of *A Midsummer Night's Dream* were staged separately as *Bottom the Weaver*. At the same time, the amateur Sir William Davenant managed to operate legitimately in 1656-58, on the basis that the operatic elements in such works as his *Siege of Rhodes* classified them as music rather than drama.

With the return of the King, however, the theatre was rapidly reorganized. Charles II issued patents for two Companies. One, under manager Thomas Killigrew, was formed from the remainder of the old King's Men company, and specialized in revivals. The other, catering for new plays, was managed by Davenant and was known as the Duke's Company. Both groups played initially in converted tennis courts until purpose-built theatres, designed by Sir Christopher Wren, were completed. Killigrew's Company settled in Drury Lane, while the Duke's theatre was in Dorset Garden, off Fleet Street.

The work of the new Companies differed in several ways from that of their predecessors under Charles I. The most obvious change was the introduction of actresses, rather than young boys, to play the female roles. In the royal patents licensing the Companies it was claimed that this was for a moral purpose – to end the dubious practice of men appearing 'in the habits of women'. But the truth was simply that Charles II had enjoyed seeing actresses on stage during his exile on the Continent. The earliest recorded appearance of a woman player in England was in *Othello*, in December 1660; Pepys first saw one soon after.

The most famous of these actresses was Nell Gwyn. Pepys met and admired her, both for her comic talent and her beauty. She was one of a number of gifted performers who caught his eye. He was also impressed by the musical skills of Moll Davis and Mrs Knipp. Mrs Knipp became a close friend, and used to take Pepys backstage to meet her fellow actresses until, not unreasonably, his wife's jealousy was aroused.

Not all were licentious, by any means. Mary Betterton was quite unfashionably chaste. So, too, was Anne Bracegirdle, the comedienne. But actresses were considered 'fair game', and when an assault was made on Anne's honour and an actor who sprang to her defence was murdered for his pains, neither crime received fit punishment.

Women were also in evidence behind the scenes. The Duchess of Newcastle had two collections of plays published in 1662 and 1668, while Katherine Philips had her tragedy *Pompey* performed in Dublin in 1663. But the first woman to earn her living as a dramatist was Aphra Behn. At least 16 of her plays were performed during her lifetime, making her more prolific than most of her male contemporaries. Her private life was as

The rivals
Thomas Killigrew (left) was one of the first theatre-managers to be granted a royal patent to mount plays again. His King's Company soon acquired a purpose-built theatre in Drury Lane. Their only rivals, the Duke's Company made do with a converted tennis-court until their new, Thames-side playhouse (above) was ready.

THE LONDON THEATRES. PLATE I.

Mr Powel and Mr Lee in the Characters of Oroonoko, & Aboan. Act 5. Scene last.

Mary Evans Picture Library

Mary Evans Picture Library

Aphra Behn
(below) A journey to Surinam in South America inspired the adventurous Mrs Behn's novel Oroonoko *(1688), later adapted for the stage (left). It was a remarkably progressive protest against slavery. She was herself a prolific playwright (as well as the King's spy in Antwerp) and survived sexist abuse and calumny to win wide acclaim. Her friends included Sir George Etherege, John Dryden, Thomas Otway and the Duke of Buckingham, who recognized in her their equal.*

been narrow and oblong, but in the new theatres fan-shaped auditoriums became possible.

Pepys noted with interest the improvements in design. He visited the Theatre Royal in Drury Lane the day after it opened, and described it as being "made with extraordinary good contrivance". This particular theatre burnt down in 1672 and was replaced with Wren's building in 1674. Pepys was particularly impressed with the improvements in stage lighting, which utilized wax rather than tallow candles. Another telling fact that emerges from his *Diary* is the ease with which members of the public could gain access to all parts of the theatre, even the actresses' dressing rooms – a facility that ensured gossip.

A DIFFERENT AUDIENCE

The Restoration theatre attracted a varied audience (from aristocrats to whores to professional people), but the drama was mainly dictated by a courtly élite. For most of Charles' reign, London had only two theatres (there had been six in the Elizabethan era). By 1682 audiences had declined to such an extent that the King's and the Duke's Companies merged into one company which performed unchallenged until 1695. The preoccupations of the plays

Mrs Behn

Fotomas

convoluted as some of her comic plots (only *The Rover* is revived nowadays) and included a period as a spy in Antwerp and a spell in debtors' prison.

The Restoration brought a significant change to the structure of the theatre itself. The main innovation was the use of painted scenery. Framed by the new proscenium arch, a number of different backdrops could be pulled across the wings during the course of a play. The variation in backdrops was lost on the patrons who sat in boxes at the side of the theatre. But they could enjoy a greater intimacy with the actors, since the action of most plays took place on the long 'apron' stage which extended into the auditorium. At first, in the converted tennis courts, this auditorium would have

Nell Gwyn
(left) The first actresses often found work and a place in society by granting sexual favours. Nell Gwyn's entrée was as mistress of Charles Hart, a famous actor. She, too, won acclaim before catching the King's roving eye.

The Merry Gang
Charles' reign, wrote Dryden, encouraged 'noble idleness' – personified by the indolent Duke of Buckingham, a playwright who gathered round him friends (right) who could supply the kind of play he enjoyed.

Augustus Egg: The Life of Buckingham/Fine Art Photographic Library

John Vanbrugh (1664-1726)
Imprisoned in France for spying, Vanbrugh (above) wrote plays, then diversified into architecture: his most famous work was Blenheim Palace (right).

were of very little interest to the common man or woman, for they were full of oblique, bitchy allusions, readily understood by the Court and people of fashion, but entirely opaque to anyone else.

The arbiters of taste among this exclusive clientele were the King's 'merry gang': men such as the Duke of Buckingham, Sir Charles Sedley, Lord Buckhurst, Henry Savile and the infamous John Wilmot, Earl of Rochester. The opinions of these men could make or break the reputation of any budding playwright. George Etherege and William Wycherley, for example, were both accepted into courtly circles on the strength of their writing. Wycherley's rise was particularly remarkable, given that his initial success had come about through his affair with the Duchess of Cleveland. He quite naturally feared the wrath of his aristocratic rival in love, the Duke of Buckingham, but fortunately the Duke declared himself 'as much in love with wit as with his kinswoman' and appointed the playwright one of his equerries.

There was a darker side to this form of patronage. Sedley had an actor beaten up for imitating his dress, and when John Dryden insulted the Earl of Rochester in print, Wilmot hired three thugs to cudgel him in an alleyway near Covent Garden.

This curious mixture of generosity and violence, wit and immorality, found its way into the plays of the Restoration. Of all these qualities, wit was prized most, providing it was achieved without apparent effort. The poet Alexander Pope called Charles II's court 'the mob of gentlemen who wrought with ease'; certainly both Sedley and Wilmot were talented writers. It was common

Restoration comedy
It is witty, wordy and largely superficial, its plots implausible and derivative. It deals in gossip, fashion, witty insult, sexual intrigue and double-dealing. Even at the time, its amorality caused controversy. Boastful Lord Foppington (seen holding court, right) is a typical Restoration character, used by two leading contemporary playwrights – Vanbrugh and Cibber. (Fops tend to head the sub-plot, while some more virile 'hero' initiates the main action.) Modern audiences miss many of the dated allusions to real people, and plays – often four hours long in the original – bear ruthless cutting in revival. But at its best, Restoration drama glitters and dazzles with wit, pace and slickness.

William Congreve (1670-1729)
*(above) The success of his comedies –
including* Love for Love *and* The
Way of the World – *owed much to the
talent of actress Anne Bracegirdle, his
lifelong friend. He virtually stopped
writing at 30 although his circle included
Swift, Steele and Pope.*

practice for members of the audience (including
the King) to suggest characters or 'improvements' in the plot. This air of courtly amateur-
ism is at the heart of Restoration comedy.

Of the five major playwrights of the period
– Etherege, Wycherley, William Congreve,
John Vanbrugh and George Farquhar – the
first three had finished writing for the
theatre when they were in their 30s, while the
fourth is far better known for his work as an
architect. Farquhar was the only professional
among them, and he died young, having
completed only eight plays.

These young men specialized in the 'comedy of
manners'. In this, the essential struggle lay not
between vice and virtue or love and honour, but
between wit and dullness. The hero was usually a
witty, aristocratic rake – often penniless and for-
tune-hunting – and the butts of his humour were
either the hypocritical Puritan, the absurd fop, the
boorish countryman or the dull and cuckolded
citizen. The archetypal characters in this vein are
Dorimant (probably based on the Earl of Rochester) in Etherege's *Man of Mode* (1676), Horner in
Wycherley's *The Country Wife* (1675) and Mirabell
in Congreve's *Way of the World* (1700).

The normal setting for their witty escapades
was London – not the City, but the highly fashionable area encompassed by the Strand, Covent

William Wycherley (1641-1715)
*Wycherley (above) fell in and out of
favour with Charles II, who finally
left him to rot in debtors' prison. But
James II, admiring his play* The Plain
Dealer *(below), took pity on him, paid
his debts and had him released.*

THE
Plain Dealer,
A
COMEDY,
As it is Acted
At the THEATRE ROYAL.

Written by Mr. WYCHERLEY.

—— *Ridiculum acri
Fortius & melius magnas plerumque secat res.*
HORAT.

LONDON:
Printed for W. FEALES, at *Rowe's Head*, against St. Cle-
ment's Church in the *Strand*; R. WELLINGTON, at
the *Dolphin and Crown*, and C. CORBETT, at *Addi-
son's Head*, both without *Temple-Bar*; J. BRINDLEY,
at the *King's Arms* in New *Bond-street*; A. BETTES-
WORTH, and F. CLAY, in Trust for B. WELLINGTON.

MDCCXXXV.

Garden and Whitehall. The urban comedies of Ben
Jonson remained popular throughout the Restoration era, as did the witty repartee of two other
Jacobean dramatists, Beaumont and Fletcher.
Shakespeare fared less well, for his work suffered
various curious adaptations. Nahum Tate produced a happy ending for *King Lear* in which Cordelia was paired off with Edgar. Dryden added
new characters to *The Tempest*, while Davenant
introduced singing, dancing witches into *Macbeth*.
These bizarre revisions may in part explain Pepys'
harsh judgement of Shakespeare: *"Romeo and Juliet
. . . a play of itself the worst that ever I heard";
"Midsummer's Night Dream the most insipid ridiculous
play that ever I saw in my life."*

good lies solely in the presence of sensual pleasure.

Nevertheless, there are elements of cutting satire and moralizing social comment in Restoration comedy. Wycherley, whose plays were called filthy and obscene, actually busied himself with exposing the faults of his age. He acquired the nickname 'Manly Wycherley' after his complex hero in *The Plain Dealer*. Captain Manly gives vent to a succession of jaundiced attacks on his generation's fashionable nihilism, perfidy, sexual hypocrisy, amoral superficiality, foppery and indifference to true merit – even if he is not above seeking vengeance himself.

RESTORATION TRAGEDY

The comedy co-existed with a vogue for highly charged heroic dramas. Their popularity, begun by Davenant's *Siege of Rhodes,* was further stimulated by the success of classical tragedy in France. In imitation of the French, English heroic dramas were frequently written in rhyming couplets. But there were no tragedies to compare with those of the great Jean Racine. Restoration tragedies, with their bombastic protestations of love and honour, are rarely revived today.

The playwrights most associated with them are

One feature retained from Elizabethan drama was the complexity of the plots, many of which were 'borrowed' shamelessly from elsewhere. (Wycherley's *The Plain Dealer* is an amalgamation of the inimitable French writer Molière's *Le Misanthrope* and Shakespeare's *Twelfth Night.*) At times, the plots became so labyrinthine that one later critic was prompted to ask, 'How could an audience both be clever enough to understand the story, and stupid enough to be interested by it when they did?' The answer was, of course, that the story was secondary to the manner of its telling. Congreve's plots might be trivial, but his sparkling dialogue ranks with the best comic writing in the English language.

A frequent criticism levelled against Restoration playwrights was their apparent cynicism and immorality. In Dr Johnson's memorable words:
"Themselves they studied, as they felt they writ;
Intrigue was plot, obscenity was wit.
Vice always found a sympathetic friend;
They pleas'd their age, and did not aim to mend."
There was a degree of truth in this. The courtiers who returned to England after 1660 were typical of a post-war generation. Often they were rootless – many estates had been lost during the Civil War – and this fact explains the abundance of impoverished, genteel fortune-hunters portrayed on stage. In addition, there was a reaction against the weighty, worthy sentiments, both Puritan and Royalist, that typified the period before the Civil War. In this climate, the pursuit of pleasure seemed the only virtue. The guru of the Restoration was the philosopher Thomas Hobbes. His hugely influential book, *Leviathan,* argued that the life of a man is naturally 'solitary, poore, nasty, brutish and short', and that the true definition of

New generation
Young Alexander Pope meets John Dryden at Will's Coffee House: a new generation growing up in qualified admiration of the one before.

Tragic loss
Most Restoration tragedies were pompous and bombastic, but a few, such as Venice Preserv'd *(right), have been deemed worthy of revival.*

Powerful prudery
Jeremy Collier, Anglican divine, denounced the titillating comedies (below). A peevish middle-class public agreed, and the heyday was over.

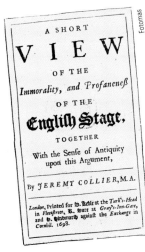

A SHORT
VIEW
OF THE
Immorality, and Profaneneß
OF THE
English Stage,
TOGETHER
With the Senſe of Antiquity
upon this Argument,

By JEREMY COLLIER, M.A.

London, Printed for S. Keble at the *Turk's-Head* in *Fleetſtreet,* R. Sare at *Gray's-Inn-Gate,* and H. Hindmarſh againſt the *Exchange* in *Cornhil.* 1698.

Dryden – whose best work lay outside the theatre, as a poet – Elkanah Settle and Nathaniel Lee. The best tragedies of the period were domestic rather than heroic. Thomas Otway's *The Orphan* (1680) and *Venice Preserv'd* (1682) achieved a genuine pathos and lasting merit.

The backlash against courtly wit began in 1698 when Jeremy Collier, an Anglican clergyman, published *A Short View of the Immorality and Profaneness of the English Stage.* Collier's belief 'that the business of plays is to recommend Virtue and discountenance Vice' met with the approval of middle-class audiences excluded from the in-jokes and snobbish egotism of the courtly plays. Although much of the work of Vanbrugh and Farquhar was still to come, the golden age of the comedy of manners was drawing to a close.

JOHN BUNYAN

←·*1628-1688*·→

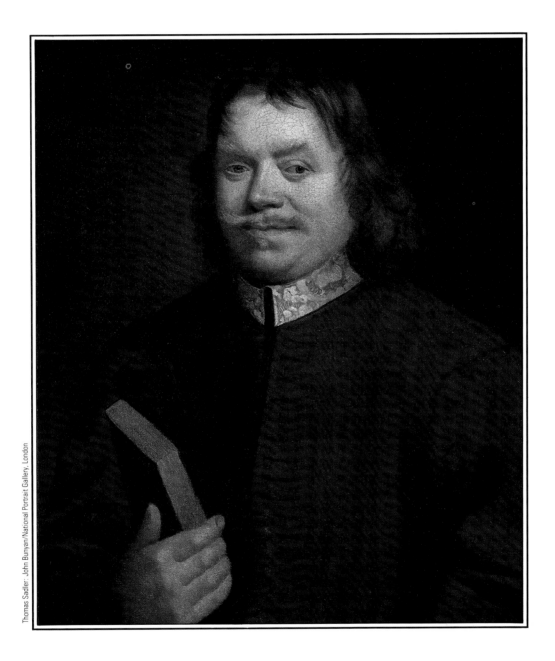

Poor and half–educated, workman John Bunyan became one
of the most widely read Christian writers – 'Father of the
Novel', as Kipling called him, and one of the 'great
creative minds' of the 17th century, in the historian
Macaulay's view. His life was full of hardship, enduring
persecution, prolonged imprisonment and an agonizing
struggle to find faith which he expressed in the glorious
poetic allegory of *The Pilgrims' Progress*.

Prisoner of Conscience

Having overcome his own spiritual crisis, John Bunyan had to fight the 'demons' of religious intolerance. Imprisoned for long periods, he found the time to write *The Pilgrim's Progress*.

Although John Bunyan professed to have come from "the meanest and most despised" of backgrounds, his ancestors were of respectable yeoman stock before the family fortunes declined. The area of his birth, Bedfordshire, was remarkably beautiful, with the River Ouse coursing through its meadows, and John Bunyan's ancestral roots ran deep there.

There had been Bunyans in the Bedford area since the 1200s. John was born at the nearby hamlet of Harrowden sometime during 1628, and baptized in Elstow parish church on November 30 that year. He was the eldest of three children; his sister, Margaret, arrived less than 12 months later, and his brother, William, in 1633.

Very little is known about John's mother, née Mary or Margaret Bentley, except that she was the second wife of his father, Thomas Bunyan. He earned his living as an itinerant brazier or tinker, mending kettles and pans, and he also worked the few acres of land he owned.

Although the family lived in modest comfort, their lives were marked by the exhausting hard work then necessary for survival. From the age of 10, John travelled the district helping his father and learning the trade. His caring but strict parents – his father beat him regularly – insisted he 'larn' to read and write. He was probably taught at a local charity school rather than the nearby grammar school. Had he received higher formal education he would have learned Latin; John was later adamant he knew nothing of it.

He may well have imbibed more than has been realized from his grandfather, a 'pettie chapman' –

A Bedfordshire lad
Born and bred in Bedfordshire, John Bunyan (below left) drew inspiration from his surroundings. He lived in a simple but comfortable house (bottom left) with his parents and younger brother and sister Margaret. He was devastated when Margaret, one year younger than him and the closest to him in his affections, died unexpectedly at 15.

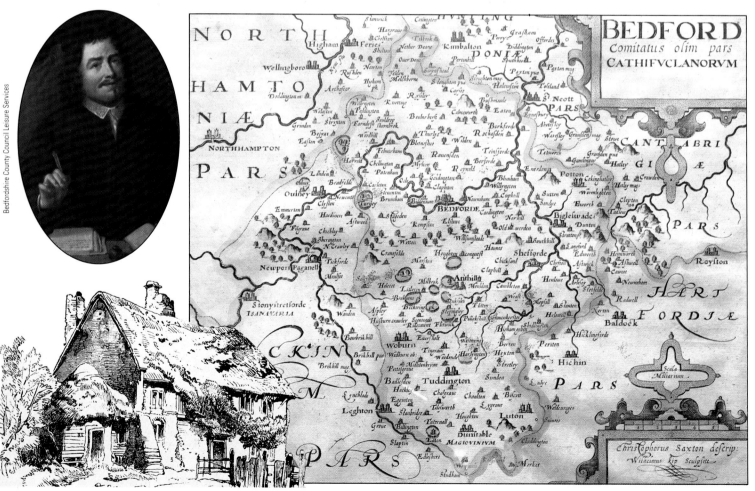

Key Dates

1628 born near Bedford

1638 starts to learn trade as tinker

1644 mother and sister die; enters army service

c.1649 marries Mary

1650 birth of blind daughter Mary; onset of emotional crisis

1653 joins separatist congregation, Bedford

1657 becomes a preacher

1658 marries Elizabeth, following Mary's death

1660 gaoled for Nonconformism

1666 *Grace Abounding*

1672 released from prison

1676–77 second term of imprisonment

1678 *The Pilgrim's Progress*

1688 dies in London

Historic Hall

The 15th-century Moot Hall (below) housed the materials for the Elstow Fayre – much in Bunyan's mind when he wrote of 'Vanity Fair'.

pedlar, or travelling salesman – whose wares included the cheap, popular 'chapbooks' full of stirring, humorous and morally uplifting tales. *St George and the Dragon* was among John's favourites; yet if the old man helped feed his intelligence and already vivid imagination, he seemed powerless to lessen the morbid effects of insecurity and repression.

John's adolescence coincided with the start of one of the apocalyptic ages in English history – a near-half-century not just of zealous Puritanism, but civil war, the beheading of a despotic king, plague, republican rule, a complete shake-up of the monarchy and finally the 'peaceful revolution' that resulted in modern democracy.

EARLY TRAUMAS

The tensions had been mounting for many years. Yet the rural scene of John's youth – the streams and wheatfields of Bedfordshire – were as yet untouched by the constitutional hurricanes brewing at Westminster. But the nationwide dogmatism that cramped personal liberties, the rigid laws that demanded religious observance, the vengeful Old Testament justice that specified slow death by hanging – all these had traumatized John's mind from an early age. The ultimate warning against sin was unavoidable; from gibbets at every major crossroads swung the tar-preserved corpses of executed 'criminals'.

"The Lord, even in my childhood, did scare and affright me with fearful dreams, and did terrify me with dreadful visions", John recorded; "I should often wish either that there had been no Hell, or that I had been a Devil . . . that I might be rather a tormenter than tormented myself."

The nightmares were those of an acutely sensitive child; in them, John was chased by demons from whom he could not escape. The terror lasted well into his adulthood, together with a further symptom of his neurosis – panic that the tower of Elstow church would fall on him.

He was also much troubled by the aggressive

Fact or Fiction

JUSTICE KELYNG

It was before the fierce, haughty Justice Kelyng that John Bunyan was tried in 1660. Unrepentant of his right to pray as and where he chose, he was found guilty as charged and sentenced to three months' imprisonment. If at the end of that time he did not go to church and stop preaching, he would be banished from the realm, and, failing that, hanged. Later Justice Kelyng starred as Lord Hategood in the trial of Faithful – one of many real-life originals in *The Pilgrim's Progress*.

Elstow Church christening

On 30 November 1628, John Bunyan made his first official appearance (below) – on his baptismal record.

reaction of "cursing, swearing and blaspheming". His guilt feelings were real enough; on existing evidence, however, the causes seem mild by present standards – nothing worse than occasional bouts of heavy drinking and visiting harlots. But John thought he had committed "all manner of vice and ungodliness".

During the summer of his sixteenth year, his mother and sister died in quick succession, possibly of some epidemic disease. Bunyan, who had been very close to them, was devastated by their loss and even more so by the speed with which his father remarried – just three months later. His grieving was cut short in November 1644, however, when he was mustered for military service. He was probably stationed with the Parliamentary garrison at Newport Pagnell. In the little action he saw, Bunyan escaped death during a siege after agreeing to change places with a sentry who was "shot into the head with a Musket bullet and died".

STRONGER IN BODY

Demobilized in 1647, Bunyan returned to Elstow, resumed work as a tinker and acquired his own cottage. Some thought him 'a rogue', but friends found him happier, more secure, less worried about religion. Large-boned and powerfully-built, he exuded youthful energy; he readily joined in village pastimes like dancing, wrestling and tipcat – a game with sticks – and took special pleasure in bell-ringing, especially his 'own' bell.

His wit, charm and appearance – he was tall and blue-eyed, with reddish-brown hair – soon won the heart of a local girl whom he had met in his army days. Her identity is unknown, but she is thought to have been named Mary. They were wed about 1649, coming together "poor as poor

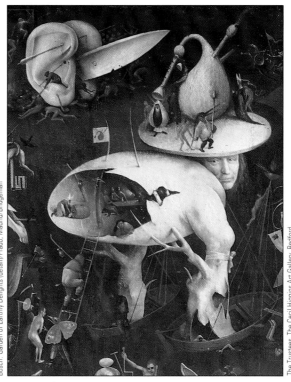

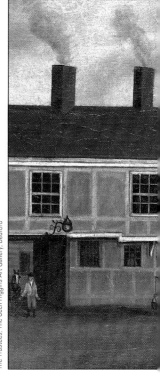

Fevered imaginings
Bunyan's childhood and young manhood were plagued by terrifying nightmares. Over and over he dreamt that he was being pursued by demonic figures, heard voices, felt devils pinching him – all in retribution for his sins . . .

Preaching the Gospel
Having found his faith, Bunyan started spreading the word of the Lord. He was an easy and humorous speaker, and drew crowds. Below he is shown preaching in front of Bedford's Guildhall in 1659, the year before he was first imprisoned.

Guilty as charged
The Swan Inn (above) was the scene of Bunyan's first trial. The assizes were held there, at which he was found guilty of 'devilishly and perniciously' boycotting divine service and 'upholding unlawful meetings'.

John and Elizabeth
After his first wife Mary had died, a friend of hers, Elizabeth (far right), married John Bunyan and took on his four children. The union was a happy one, although never easy. John spent 12 years of their married life in prison, but Elizabeth proved herself a strong and loyal ally, always campaigning for his release.

might be, not having so much household-stuff as a Dish or Spoon betwixt us both".

Gentle and God-fearing, Mary brought with her two popular, pious books, *The Plaine Man's Pathway to Heaven,* and *The Practice of Piety,* which she and John sometimes read together. They were happy, the marriage was successful, and the first of their four children – Mary – was born in 1650. She was born blind, a tragedy which aroused John's intense pity – and guilt; he believed his infant daughter was being punished for his sins.

GIANT DESPAIR

Bunyan began to experience black depressions ("Giant Despair") in which he felt caged, worthless, contemptible. He heard voices; one Sunday afternoon, he wrote, a call "did suddenly dart from Heaven into my Soul" during a game of tipcat on Elstow Green. He saw "the Lord Jesus looking down upon me, as being very hotly displeased . . ."

Disembodied voices can be a classic symptom of schizophrenia, one reason for the mistaken assumption that Bunyan was a psychotic, even psychopathic personality; in Bunyan's case, the voices were echoes of unconscious thoughts apparently so clear as to belong to the real world. Certainly, he became almost demented, near-suicidal with self-loathing; but valiant "'Gainst all disaster", he clung doggedly to reason and hope, buoyed at times by little more than an animal will to live and, with Mary's encouragement, an awareness that his salvation might lie in embracing the very God who had oppressed him.

There were no psychiatrists to help. Bunyan had to work out for himself that personal demons are defeated by direct confrontation. But if the worst

of the paranoid conflict was resolved, he now struggled to find fresh meaning and purpose: "My soul is as a clog on the leg of a Bird", he lamented to a group of women sitting in the sun on a Bedford doorstep. They spoke to him of rebirth, of their wretchedness without Christ's love: "They spake as if joy did make them speak", Bunyan said; "they were to me as if they had found a new world".

It was a major turning-point. Bunyan renewed his Bible studies and became friends with John Gifford, a reformed drunkard who was pastor of the newly-formed Independent Congregation which met at St John's Church in Bedford.

Bunyan joined the Congregation in the early 1650s and moved his family to a three-room cottage in Bedford, then inhabited by only 2000 people. After further crises, he finally found

Lenient punishment
Although lengthy and arduous (notice the leg chains), Bunyan's time in prison was very productive. He did much of his best writing there and, by contemporary standards, was well treated. His family and friends were allowed to visit him, and he was granted occasional 'conjugal visits' to his home and one home-cooked meal a day, possibly delivered by his blind daughter Mary.

Southwark Meeting House
After his release from prison, John returned to his preaching, travelling around the eastern counties and holding gatherings at Southwark Meeting House (left) in London.

Travelling preacher
The contemporary print below shows Bunyan, now famous, being hailed by an elderly passer-by.

true faith, gaining confidence in himself as some-one lovable in the sight of God.

But nothing could save his poor wife Mary. Prematurely worn out after 10 years of marriage, she died soon after the birth of their son Thomas, in 1658. John was shattered; Hell re-opened its gates. But there were now four children to look after and grief had to be put aside. Within a year John married again. His second wife, Elizabeth, had been a friend of Mary's, but was by all accounts a stronger personality. She loved John and his children dearly; it was a love well returned.

Her love, however, was soon to be sorely tested. Following Cromwell's death and the restoration of Charles II to the throne, the State attempted to achieve national unity by legislating for religious uniformity. Nonconformist preaching was outlawed.

TAKEN INTO CUSTODY

Bunyan, by now renowned as a virile, humorous, direct speaker, refused to be silenced. A warrant for his arrest was issued in November 1660. He gave himself up at Samsell, near Harlington, was taken before a furious local magistrate, and remanded in custody to await trial.

At the Quarter Sessions seven weeks later, he was indicted with "devilishly and perniciously" abstaining from attending divine service and "upholding unlawful meetings".

According to Statute, Bunyan was guilty on both counts, though the trial degenerated into a class feud. He defied the judges, who sneered that he was "a canting pedlar". Justice Kelyng ordered him to be "had back to prison, and there to lie for three months"; if he then continued to flout the law, he would "stretch by the neck for it". After 90 days, Bunyan was asked if he would consent to be ruled. He adamantly insisted on the right to free speech and action.

It was the start of 12 years' imprisonment. Elizabeth, who had miscarried just before the trial, tried bravely, repeatedly, to have the case reopened. Responding to her plea, the House of Lords recommended Bunyan's release. The advice was ignored.

The immediate effect of confinement on a man liable to panic attacks – a man, moreover, who thrived on exercise and open-air pursuits – can only be guessed at; worse, it seems, was the "parting from my Wife and poor Children". He was held at the County Gaol, less than five minutes' walk from his home.

Since Bunyan was a prisoner of conscience, not a common criminal, several privileges were granted. His family and friends were permitted to visit him, and to send in one meal a day. Tradition tells that his blind daughter Mary came daily with

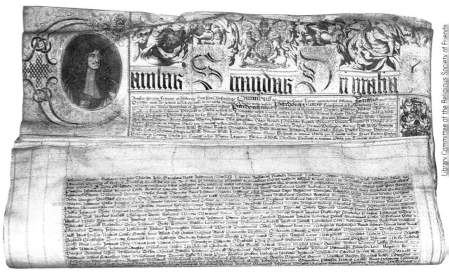

a jug of soup or ale. John supported the family by making and selling bootlaces. He was occasionally allowed out on conjugal excursions. In prison, most of his time was devoted to writing; he completed several books, including his life-story *Grace Abounding to the Chief of Sinners,* and he started writing *The Pilgrim's Progress.*

Bunyan was freed in 1672 on the King's Declaration of Religious Indulgence, and immediately appointed minister of the Independent Congregation, which bought a barn and orchard on Bedford's Mill Street for conversion into their place of worship. The same year, Elizabeth gave birth to a son, Joseph.

Royal Charter of Freedom
Bunyan was released from prison in 1672 following the King's Declaration of Religious Indulgence (above). Unfortunately, four years later this was withdrawn and Bunyan – as well as all others considered guilty of Nonconformist beliefs or actions – was returned to prison.

Now fully occupied as the Congregation's leader, John enjoyed four years' uneasy freedom before being returned to prison following withdrawal of the King's Declaration. He was released in June 1677. His greatest masterpiece, *The Pilgrim's Progress,* was published on 18 February the following year.

"Some said, 'John, print it'; others said 'Not so'", Bunyan recalled. *The Pilgrim's Progress from this World to that which is to come* sold at 1s 6d (7½p) and was a resounding national success; 11 editions totalling 100,000 copies – a massive sale for its time – appeared over the next decade. It has since been translated into more than 200 languages.

His publisher Nathaniel Ponder made a fortune. Bunyan probably sold the work outright and earned very little money himself. This doubtless caused friction between the men, although Bunyan's driving forces had been artistic and spiritual; he sought only to do the greatest good, and to share his creed that "Faith dissolves Doubts, as the Sun drives away the Mists".

A POPULAR HERO

Like his central character, Christian, he had suffered for a cause and survived to be hailed as a hero. 'Bishop Bunyan' took a childlike delight in this recognition yet continued to live humbly, teaching and preaching his gospel in London and the Eastern counties, retreading the landscape he had transformed – Stevington Cross, for instance, where Christian supposedly shed his burden; and Millbrook Gorge, near Ampthill – the dragon-haunted Valley of the Shadow of Death.

During the last 10 years of his life, Bunyan wrote a

further 40 books, including *The Life and Death of Mr Badman* and *The Holy War.* He died in London (where he had gone to preach) on 31 August 1688, probably of pneumonia contracted after riding 40 miles through a rainstorm, and was buried in Bunhill Fields cemetery in the City of London.

His meagre estate, valued at just £42 19s., went to Elizabeth. Heartbroken that the trumpets had finally sounded for her beloved husband, she followed him to the grave soon after.

Earthly resting place
Bunyan is reputed to have died at the house of his friend John Strudwick (left) – the 'Holborn Grocer'. According to a contemporary account, he was travelling to London when, after riding out of his way to settle a quarrel between a father and son, he was 'overtaken with excessive rains, coming to his lodgings extream wet, and fell sick of a violent feavor'. He was buried in the Strudwicks' family grave in Bunhill Fields cemetery (below) in the City of London.

BEDFORDSHIRE

Many places in Bunyan's native Bedfordshire found their way into *The Pilgrim's Progress:* the fertile plain near Ampthill was transformed into the Slough of Despond; Stevington Cross became the Wicket Gate where Christian shed his burden; St John's Rectory, where Bunyan and Gifford discussed religion, re-emerged as the Interpreter's House; the Jacobean Houghton House (below) was the House Beautiful and Milbrook Gorge inspired the Valley of the Shadow of Death.

THE PILGRIM'S PROGRESS

An autobiographical allegory about Man's path from sin to salvation, Bunyan's masterwork still has a strong appeal for its astute and witty observation of human nature.

The Pilgrim's Progress is the most famous and most popular allegory in English literature. By definition, an allegory is a limited literary form, since characters are used to exhibit abstract concepts or moral qualities and the plot takes a predictably didactic course. Yet Bunyan manages to infuse his story with the narrative power of a novel, including all the key components that make up a fine work of fiction – contrast, variety, excitement, realism, sense of place, alert observation of character. Another original feature of the book is the way it blurs the line between allegory and autobiography, since it is a stylized account of Bunyan's own religious conversion. Although not published until 1678, it seems likely that he began writing it during one of his spells of imprisonment for preaching illegally. Far from closing his mouth, prison seems to have inspired him.

Like many great works of literature, from Cervantes' *Don Quixote* through Twain's *Huckleberry Finn* to Steinbeck's *Grapes of Wrath*, *The Pilgrim's Progress* is structured around the idea of a physical journey that also becomes a spiritual voyage. Wearing rags that are a symbol of man's earthly poverty, and feeling a burden of guilt upon him, Bunyan's hero Christian is given a parchment roll by Evangelist which has written on it the words, "Fly from the wrath to come". Christian's journey from the City of Destruction to the Celestial City encapsulates the theme of the book, which is the progress of the soul from sin to salvation. The obstacles he encounters are the temptations and tribulations everyone must face on a quest to enter Heaven.

GUIDE TO THE PLOT

Christian is deaf to the entreaties of his wife and family to stay: "the Man put his fingers in his ears and ran on, crying, Life! Life! Eternal Life!". And a neighbour, Pliable, who is tempted to follow him, is so disturbed by the experience of crossing the Slough of Despond that he turns back. Yet, although determined, Christian is still naive, and can be diverted from the true path by such characters as Mr

"Life! Eternal Life!"
Christian, quitting wife and children (above) in pursuit of salvation, recalls Christ's warning that faith may break the closest family bonds.

Slough of Despond
Christian falls into despair (because of his burden of sin). But Help pulls him out (right).

Wordly-Wiseman, who beguiles him with facile advice and professes to know a better way for Christian to shed his burden. However, after being chastised by Evangelist and re-directed to the Wicket Gate (the symbol of Christ) through which he passes, Christian is given renewed heart at the Interpreter's House. Climbing up the highway by a Wall called Salvation and coming to a Cross, Christian finds that just as he "came up with the

Cross, his burden loosed from off his shoulders and fell from off his back". There is now no personal impediment to his journey. "I must venture", he says, "To go back is nothing but death; to go forward is fear of death and life everlasting beyond it."

From here, the dangers that Christian will face come mainly in two forms: the threat of hypocrisy and shallow faith posed by characters such as By-Ends; and the more formidable enemy of spiritual despair, as represented by Apollyon and Giant Despair. The earlier struggles tend to be more elemental and violent, like the fight with Apollyon in the Valley of Humiliation. "In this Combat no man can imagine, unless he had seen and heard as I did, what yelling and hideous roaring Apollyon made all the time of the fight . . . ". The conflicts in the later stages of the journey tend to be more subtle and psychological, like Christian's momen-

tary lack of faith when crossing the River of Death. "These troubles and distresses that you go through in these Waters are no sign that God hath forsaken you", Hopeful reminds him, "but are sent to try you . . ."

At times, then, as when he vanquishes the monster Apollyon, Christian appears as a hero of romance with sword and armour. At other times, as when he escapes with Hopeful from imprisonment

'. . . and my burden is light'
As Christian nears the Cross (above), his burden of sin falls from his back making everything easier afterwards.

by Giant Despair, his weapons are prayer and a key called Promise that goes into the lock of Doubting-Castle.

During the journey, Christian meets up with fellow pilgrim Faithful, and both reach Vanity Fair: "He that will go to the City, and yet not go through this Town, must needs go out of the world." Bunyan offers Vanity Fair as a symbol of corrupt materialism that might trap and capture man's soul. Although Christian and Faithful are not tempted, their dress,

"The Valley of the Shadow of Death"
(below) In this fearful place lurk whispering Demons and "snares, traps, gins and nets", as well as a quagmire and two giants.

Apollyon the Devil
"The angel of the bottomless pit", whose name means 'destroyer', has finally to be confronted (right).

"Pliable. Then said Pliable, Don't revile; if what the good Christian says is true, the things he looks after are better than ours; my heart inclines to go with my neighbour. Obstinate. What! more fools still? Be ruled by me and go back. Who knows whither such a brain-sick fellow will lead you? Go back, go back, and be wise."

speech and unworldliness arouse the derision of the godless. Fights ensue, and they are imprisoned and brought to trial.

The trial scene is one of the great set-pieces of the novel, undoubtedly inspired by Bunyan's own experience of arrest and examination before justices. The Judge is called Lord Hategood and the false witnesses against Christian and Faithful include Envy and Superstition. Indeed, in an astute touch, Envy starts eagerly on his complaint against the pilgrims before he has even been sworn in. Mr Blind-man is the Foreman of the Jury. "I see clearly that this Man is a Heretic", he says of Faithful, and Faithful is condemned to "the most cruel death that could be invented" before his soul is transported to the Celestial Gate. It is a reminder of the toughness of the book and its unsentimentality about religious persecution.

Christian is joined by Hopeful and suffers under Giant Despair, but his opponents begin to assume less formidable forms – in the blandishments of Flattery, the contempt of Atheism, the apprehension of False-Fear, until the gripping final crossing of the River of Death.

PERILOUS JOURNEY

An allegory on the theme of religious salvation would seem to have a relatively specialized literary appeal, yet *The Pilgrim's Progress* has become a popular classic. From the gripping opening sentence onwards ("As I walked through the wil-

'Vanity of vanities'
All is vanity in the town (below) whose Fair has run for 5,000 years.

Bedfordshire County Council Leisure Services

derness of this world, I lighted on a certain place where there was a Den, and I laid me down in that place to sleep; and as I slept I dreamed a Dream") Bunyan's talent is plain. The allegorical journey was an ideal form for him to express his thoughts. It fits his vision of life as a perilous journey with the reward of Heaven at the end for the worthy, and it gains a particular intensity from its basis in personal experience. Christian is a kind of self-portrait, reflecting many of Bunyan's own characteristics and experiences. Like Bunyan, for example, Christian has four

'Faithful unto death'
After his torture and death (above), Faithful is borne away to heaven in a chariot (like Elijah).

Giant Despair
The gaoler at Doubting-Castle (right) is told by his wife to urge suicide on his prisoners.

Mansell Collection

children and like the author, he is imprisoned because of his religious convictions. So the pilgrim's progress seems not an abstract and detached tale of a two-dimensional figure, but feels like a raw reconstruction of Bunyan's own voyage of self-discovery and self-adjustment.

If *The Pilgrim's Progress* gains some of its power from its sense of personal authenticity, another factor is Bunyan's skill as a natural allegorist. He achieves a judicious balance between the abstract and the individual, the romantic and the real. On one level, the story is a kind of holy fairy-tale that is full of giants, quagmires, imprisonment, the magic key, and so forth. It is probably this element of the story that made it ideal reading for children and, while Bunyan never talks down to his audience, there is about the narra-

Delectable Mountains
Four shepherds – Knowledge, Sincere, Watchful and Experience – greet the pilgrims with the news that they are already in 'Immanuel's Land'. It is still possible to go astray from their narrow path, but through a perspective glass (telescope) they are able to catch a first glimpse of the Celestial City from the crest of the hill called Clear.

"Then went the jury out, whose names were Mr Blindman, Mr No-good, Mr Malice, Mr Love-lust, Mr Live-loose, Mr Heady, Mr High-mind, Mr Enmity, Mr Liar, Mr Cruelty, Mr Hate-light, and Mr Implacable, who every one gave in his private verdict against him among themselves, and afterwards unanimously concluded to bring him in guilty before the Judge."

tive a childlike wonder and innocence.

Underpinning the fantasy, however, is a realism of detail and expression that gives this fairy-tale a contemporary immediacy. Bunyan is obviously more immediately accessible as a religious writer than, for example, Milton, for he tells his story from the point of view of the average man, and indeed gives a dignity to the lowly life that is not to be matched in English literature until Wordsworth. The narration is full of charmingly colloquial phrases – "I was musing in the midst of my dumps", "changed a bad for the worse", and so on. Also the adventures are not too removed from reality. The road Christian travels is one that an Englishman of the seventeenth

century would have recognized – often flooded, plagued by highwaymen. The realism is intensified by Bunyan's shrewd sense of humanity. His close psychological attention to Christian's state of mind as he crosses the River of Death – the vacillation between hope and horror, determination and despair – is a masterly portrayal of the feelings that must credibly pass through anyone's mind when faced with death.

Ultimately, however, *The Pilgrim's Progress* transcends its seventeenth-century origins and gathers a fresh application to each new century. No one could dispute the universality of Bunyan's majestic story-telling, nor of his instinctive understanding of human nature.

| In the Background |

ORIGINAL SIN

Original sin is the name given to the theological notion that all human beings are innately wicked because of Adam and Eve's fall from grace. The fact that they disobeyed God by eating the apple means that none of their descendants can account themselves innocent of sin. It is only through God's grace that some are chosen to go to Heaven. As a child, Bunyan had strong fears of Hell and believed the Calvinist doctrine that only the elected few could escape damnation. Although this is a book about Heaven, the flames of Hell flicker in the background, ready to engulf the unwary.

CHARACTERS IN FOCUS

The poet Coleridge said of Bunyan's characters that he thought of them not so much as allegorical figures as 'real persons who had been nicknamed by their neighbours'. For the most part they embody single vices or virtues, but some become individuals, their characters revealed by novelistic devices such as naturalist dialogue and humour.

WHO'S WHO

Christian   The pilgrim hero who flees from the City of Destruction and encounters many perils on his journey to the Celestial City.

Evangelist   Christian's guide who represents the authority of the Bible.

Obstinate   A neighbour who tries to hold Christian back.

Pliable   A neighbour who follows Christian but gives up at the Slough of Despond.

Mr Worldly-Wiseman   A man from the town of Carnal Policy who tempts Christian from the righteous path.

The Interpreter   He draws useful lessons for Christian from the pictures in his house.

Apollyon   The foul fiend in the Valley of Humiliation.

Faithful   Christian's loyal companion on the pilgrimage, sentenced to a cruel death at Vanity Fair.

Talkative   "A false pilgrim, he is a tall man and something more comely at a distance than at hand."

By-Ends   A worldly character, he is only interested in religion for personal gain.

Giant Despair   Owner of Doubting Castle, he imprisons the pilgrims.

Hopeful   Christian's new, young companion after the death of Faithful.

Ignorance   "A very brisk lad" from the Country of Conceit, he is barred from the Celestial City.

Mansell Collection

The character of Christian (left) is gradually revealed through the conflicts he undergoes, and by his encounters with other characters who reflect elements of his personalit Bunyan paints a picture o single-minded man, determined to live accord to his faith, and a man of genuine sincerity who ha particular hatred of hypocrisy. He is brave, bu sometimes impulsive and easily led, and prone to moods of depression. Bu avoids idealizing him, but does suggest how he deve in understanding, so that when Hopeful appears as younger disciple, Christia able to speak with the voi of experience.

Bedfordshire County Council Leisure Services

Mr Worldly-Wiseman (left) is someone Bunyan would have been well acquainted with. He is the kind of man who tried to dissuade Bunyan from preaching and get him to obey the law rather than face imprisonment. In the story "he looked a gentleman" and seems sympathetic: "How now, good fellow, whither away after this burdened manner?" But the sympathy and advice he offers are banal and materialistic. He even offers to let Christian a house in the Village of Morality "at reasonable rates". His worldliness is quite unsuited to Christian's needs and he reveals himself, little by little, through his own words, to be a pompous, patronising bourgeois.

Mansell Collection

Faithful (above) makes an interesting contrast to Christian. Because he is less proud and less morbidly preoccupied with his own guilt and weaknesses, he is susceptible to different temptations. He has no difficulty in crossing the Slough of Despond. But as a sensual man he is sorely tempted by Madam Wanton. A simpler man than Christian, he is more disconcerted by Shame and Discontent who taunt him as dishonourable and "unmanly" and say he looks ridiculous in the eyes of the world. His brutal fate at Vanity Fair has both political and religious overtones, for Faithful is a subversive whose goodness could undermine the authorities if he is not silenced.

Three times Evangelist (left) appears to Christian – firstly he warns him of the judgement to come and directs him towards the Wicket Gate leading to Salvation; secondly he upbraids Christian for heeding the advice of Mr Worldly-Wiseman; thirdly he forewarns Christian and Faithful of their sufferings at Vanity Fair and prophesies their eventual Heavenly reward.

His name, which means 'the bringer of good news', marks out his allegorical function. In him is defined the true role of preacher: to proclaim and interpret the Gospel message, showing the way to escape the wrath of God on the Day of Judgement.

Ignorance (below) is the most controversial allegorical figure in the book. Some critics feel that his fate is unduly harsh and even that he speaks more common sense than anyone else. Bunyan's description of him, however, is as "a very brisk lad" from the Country of Conceit. His major flaws of character, in the author's eyes, are plainly his superficiality and glibness. He joins the journey at a late stage and is brimming with complacency and over-confidence. "I take my pleasure in walking alone", he says, implying a conceited self-sufficiency, a dangerous vanity and a lack of Christian humility. Thus he arrives at the Celestial Gate by a circuitous route and cannot prove his Calling. His consequent consignment to Hell brings Bunyan's tale to a shocking end. "Then they took him up, and carried him through the air to the door that I saw in the side of Hell, and put him in there. Then I saw that there was a way to Hell even from the Gates of Heaven, as well as from the City of Destruction."

SPREADING THE WORD

Having found his faith, John Bunyan saw himself as a bearer of the truth – helping others 'walk through the wilderness of the world' – but never as a 'great' writer.

Bunyan was delighted by the favourable reception of *The Pilgrim's Progress,* and in the jingling verses prefacing the Second Part he naively boasts that "so comely doth my Pilgrim walk,/That of him thousands daily sing and talk". Yet he would have been taken aback to hear himself described by posterity as 'a writer' (let alone 'a great writer') rather than as a witness to the truth. What we now think of as Bunyan's literary work was simply one aspect of his ministry – a medium through which he could extend his traditional pastoral duties of converting, comforting or fortifying those who heard or read his words. As Bunyan himself succinctly put it, 'My end – thy good.'

Of the 60 works published by Bunyan, almost all were revised and expanded sermons or controversial pamphlets. Most modern readers concentrate on a handful of books – the two parts of *The Pilgrim's*

An author's imagination
Bunyan is immersed in his vision in this frontispiece to The Pilgrim's Progress.

Progress, The Life and Death of Mr Badman, The Holy War and *Grace Abounding to the Chief of Sinners.*

Grace Abounding is the harrowing story of Bunyan's spiritual perplexities, and is written in a confessional mode that was quite common among Puritans; Bunyan's only distinction in this field was that he wrote more powerfully and vividly than his fellow-divines. The other three titles comprise his entire 'fictional' output; but Bunyan's aim in publishing them was no more 'literary' than it was in the case of his other works. *The Pilgrim's Progress* was issued in order to set others on their way: "This book", declares Bunyan, "will make a traveller of thee".

PURE INSPIRATION

This intended purpose is particularly interesting in view of the way Bunyan came to write *The Pilgrim's Progress.* According to his own account it was a work of pure inspiration: when he had almost finished a pamphlet about the 'saints' (Puritan activists) of his own time, he "Fell suddenly into an allegory/ About their journey, and the way to glory". The material shaped itself into a separate book, which Bunyan worked on without any conscious intention of publishing it.

The book was in a sense a diversion – perhaps from the tedium of prison life – but Bunyan's total absorption in his religious calling ensured that it would be as didactic as any of his other writings. However, his unconscious mind had been liberated in some mysterious fashion, and his preoccupation with spiritual experience came out in the form of a story – rather to his own bewilderment, it seems, since he wrote that "I only thought to make I know not what".

Evidently Bunyan was a fluent writer who enjoyed his work: he "set pen to paper with delight", and before he had put down his ideas "I twenty more had in my crown". Later, describing the writing of *The Holy War,* he declared that "It came from mine own heart, so to my head,/ Then to my pen, from whence immediately/ On paper I did dribble it daintily"!

Journey to the Celestial City
In The Pilgrim's Progress *Man's struggle from sin to salvation is represented as a journey, beset by obstacles. This was not a new concept – the journey metaphor had been used in literature since before the Bible.*

This appears to suggest that Bunyan was a 'natural' writer – an impression reinforced by his colloquial, unliterary style; in *Grace Abounding* he aimed to be "plain and simple, and lay down the thing as it was". This talent was partly a matter of cultural background, since Bunyan the

and for all his genius and originality, he is unmistakably a part of that tradition. In particular, his 'plain' style was not peculiar to him, but was used even by highly educated Puritans, who viewed with suspicion the rhetorical magnificence of language associated with their enemies in the Established Church.

Bunyan's subjects and story-telling techniques were also deeply grounded in tradition. The image of life as a journey or pilgrimage, found in many cultures, is older than the Bible (where Bunyan found

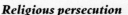

Religious persecution
Nonconformist sects – Ranters, Seekers, Quakers – suffered persecution in the 17th century (below) when only preachers licensed by the High Church, and the English Prayer Book, were sanctioned. Bunyan himself was imprisoned in Bedford gaol (above).

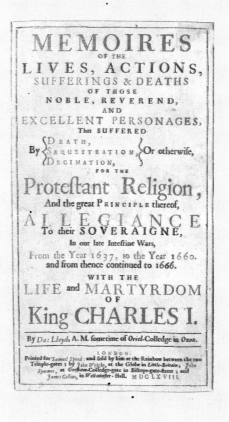

Military service
In 1644 John Bunyan was conscripted for three years' service – probably with the Parliamentary Army. Here he first encountered religious dissenters and agitators who questioned the authority of Church and Army.

tinker can have had little contact with the 'classical' education indispensable to a gentleman, and was therefore free from the temptation to invoke the Muses, quote Roman poets, or employ elaborate rhetorical devices. On the other hand, Bunyan was saturated in the rich Jacobean prose of the King James Bible, from which his characters constantly quote or borrow phrases.

There was a well-established Puritan tradition in writing with which Bunyan must have come into contact once religion had become the central concern of his life;

BUNYAN'S DIVINE EMBLEMS

1 Fish in the Water — 2. The Fowler — 3. The Lord's Prayer — 4. The Vine Tree — 5. Over-much niceness — 6. Child & Bird.
7. Boy & Butterfly — 8. Fly at the candle.

one of his locations, the Valley of the Shadow of Death) and occurs in English writing from early times. To take just one example, in the famous 15th-century play *Everyman*, the chief character, Everyman himself, is summoned by Death to make his final journey. The action mainly concerns his attempts to persuade Fellowship, Kindred, Goods, Beauty and other fair-weather friends to accompany him, and his discovery that only Good Deeds would go with him into the grave.

Everyman, like *The Pilgrim's Progress*, is an allegory, peopled with 'characters' who represent abstract ideas or types. The technique had a long history, but by Bunyan's time it was fast becoming obsolete. Nevertheless he was able to use it to immense effect in all his imaginative writings because he could make abstractions seem like real people without losing anything of their larger meaning. Mercy, for example, speaks as a self-respecting young woman who takes pride in her appearance, as well as an abstract virtue. When she shrugs off the desertion of her suitor, Mr Brisk, she declares: "I might have had husbands afore now, though I spake not of it to any; but they were such as did not like my conditions, though never did any of them find fault with my

Prolific writer

Although The Pilgrim's Progress *(above left) is the most famous of his writings, Bunyan delighted contemporary readers with many other works, such as the* Divine Emblems, *verses for children (above).*

person. So they and I could not agree."

Bunyan's great achievement was thus to bring allegory alive, using the novelist's gift for creating characters, injecting humour into situations, and giving his work a lively contemporary feel-

ing. Mr Fearing had "a Slough of Despond in his mind; a slough that he carried everywhere with him, or else he could never have been as he was"; Mr Talkative is neatly summed up as "a tall man, and something more comely at a distance than at hand"; and Great-heart praises Honest in familiar terms as "a cock of the right kind".

In a sense Bunyan's writings are transitional works, developing beyond the older forms and moving some way towards the novel as it emerged in the

18th century. But they also have their own special advantages, which help to explain their enduring appeal: with much of the humour, character and incident of a novel, they also possess a high heroic quality, biblical in its starkness and intensity, that Bunyan's novelist successors inevitably sacrificed in their careful investigations of men, manners and morals in society. For this reason Bunyan's works are, without exaggeration, unique – like nothing before or after them, and with no competitors in their own time.

Although his style and subject matter were very much in the Puritan tradition, Bunyan was responsible for a radical innovation in making a fictional story and characters absolutely central (rather than incidental) to a didactic religious work. Puritans had never been quite sure that imagined narratives really amounted to anything more than a pack of lies, and they feared that interesting stories might obscure rather than illuminate any religious message.

Bunyan was worried enough by such objections to answer them in the 'Apology' attached to the Second Part of *The Pilgrim's Progress*. He protests that Holy

International fame
John Bunyan's fame spanned continents, cultures and centuries. His statue (above) was unveiled in 1874 during the Bunyan festival in Bedford. The Matabeleland edition (left) presents The Pilgrim's Progress *in Zulu – one of over 200 languages and dialects into which it has been translated.*

Writ is full of "Dark figures, allegories" and asserts the seriousness of his intentions: "must I needs want solidness, because/ By metaphors I speak? Were not God's laws,/ His gospel laws, in olden times held forth/ By types, shadows, and metaphors?" Finally he assures the reader of his orthodoxy: his book "seems a novelty, and yet contains/ Nothing but sound and honest gospel strains". Bunyan's insistence suggests that he may have been criticized or expected criticism on this score.

ENORMOUS SUCCESS
The verdict of the world at large was quite clear, however. During Bunyan's lifetime no fewer than 11 editions of *The Pilgrim's Progress* were published; the book crossed the Atlantic to fortify the Puritan faith of the New Englanders; and it was translated into Welsh, French and Dutch.

In the 19th century Bunyan's work passed over cultural as well as linguistic boundaries: missionaries translated it into the tongues of 'savages' who knew nothing of Puritanism, the 17th century, or life in the West, and found that they too responded to a narrative in which existence is portrayed as a dangerous but momentous journey. This potent appeal has endured into the 20th century, outliving Bunyan's theology and ensuring his place among the great writers.

Allegorical figures
Allegories were often used in religious tracts for didactic purposes. The figures normally remained colourless, illustrating only one vice or virtue each – such as Simplicity, Sloth or Presumption (left). Bunyan, however, managed to breathe life into his figures, investing them with personalities and recognizable human traits which raised them beyond the confines of mere educational devices. At the same time, their simplicity and stature keeps Bunyan's message clear.

Once converted to what he believed to be the truth, John Bunyan became a prolific writer of skilful, passionately committed pamphlets and other religious works. But it seems to have been his long imprisonment that liberated his creative genius. In *Grace Abounding to the Chief of Sinners* (1666) he presents the harrowing details of his mental torments and his ultimate conviction of salvation with a vividness that sets the book apart from the mass of similar 17th-century Puritan autobiographies.

His masterpiece, *The Pilgrim's Progress* (1678), is a 'fiction' in which Bunyan uses allegory to extraordinary effect, giving life to abstractions and dramatizing clashes between the spirit and its enemies in a fashion that thrilled contemporaries and still grips readers today, whatever their religious beliefs.

The Life and Death of Mr Badman (1680) charts the 'progress' of a sinner in a small country town of the sort that Bunyan knew intimately, whereas *The Holy War* (1682) forges an exciting tale of sieges and battles out of the familiar military metaphors employed in religious discourse. By this time Bunyan was famous as the author of *The Pilgrim's Progress*, and in 1684 he published a continuation, *Part II*, in which Christian's wife undertakes the same perilous journey. The book represents a generous tribute to the Puritan woman, and is written in a less anguished spirit than Bunyan's earlier work; its mood probably reflects the more tolerant atmosphere of the times and the mellowing that age, peace and success had brought to Bunyan himself.

THE LIFE AND DEATH OF MR BADMAN

◆ 1680 ◆

Even as a youth, Badman (below) is a disgrace to his parents, lying, stealing, swearing and scorning the Sabbath. He is a worthless apprentice and keeps bad company – the perfect counterpoint to Christian in *The Pilgrim's Progress*. Hypocritically pretending to reform, he marries a pious woman whose money he can squander on lechery and drink. Again and again Badman avoids worldly disaster by committing new sins – faking bankruptcy, cheating his customers. Sickness prompts repentance but not for long, and after his wife dies he marries a notorious whore. Finally, worn out by this lifelong 'pilgrimage' towards damnation, he dies 'quietly as a lamb'.

Mansell Collection

THE HOLY WAR

◆ 1682 ◆

The 'war' between good and evil (below) is the subject of this complex allegory on the progress of the soul and the story of the Fall. The town of Mansoul (man's soul) is laid siege to by Diabolus (the Devil). After Captain Resistance dies, morale crumbles and the gates (Eye-gate, Ear-gate) are opened. Shaddai (God) sends an army to the rescue, with Prince Emmanuel (Jesus) at its head. Diabolus is taken away in chains. But although the Prince forgives the town's collaborators, Carnal Security now wins over the people. The offended Prince withdraws, leaving them prey to Diabolus again. The citizens are doomed – unless Emmanuel relents . . .

GRACE ABOUNDING TO THE CHIEF OF SINNERS

✦ 1666 ✦

Temptations of the flesh (left) beset men and women all life long, and in this spiritual autobiography, written in prison, Bunyan recounts his excruciatingly painful struggles with sin, doubt and despair. During childhood he is haunted by dreams of Hell-fire, yet he develops into a wild young man. He fails to reform his life until a heavenly voice warns him against playing games on the Sabbath, and a woman's rebuke breaks him of the ingrained habit of swearing. But though now conventionally pious, Bunyan remains dissatisfied until he encounters a group of poor women sitting on a door-step in the sunlight, talking about religion with a simple certainty. His vision of himself in the freezing cold, squeezing through a gap in the wall into the sunshine, points the way forward. However, there are still many dark years of inner torment ahead of him before he can finally be assured of God's love and eternal salvation.

THE PILGRIM'S PROGRESS PART II

✦ 1684 ✦

Christian's wife, Christiana, is roused to regret the way she treated her husband (above) and determines to make her own pilgrimage to the Celestial City. She sets out with her four sons and one other woman, Mercy. Along the way they find a protector in Mr Great-heart who defeats the Giants Grim, Maul and even Despair. En route, the children grow up: the eldest marries. After many familiar encounters, led by Christiana, the weary pilgrims cross the final river to enter the gates of the Celestial City.

The Civil War

The English Civil War pitched King against Parliament, Cavaliers against Roundheads, Puritans against Anglicans, brother against brother.

John Bunyan was thirteen years old when, in 1642, England entered one of the most traumatic, convulsive periods in its history. For nine years, the country was torn apart by bloody and bitter civil war as the King and Parliament struggled for ascendancy. By the time it was over, Bunyan was a grown man, and his life was profoundly changed.

The origins of this struggle are complex and still fiercely disputed even today. Some see it as the painful birth of capitalist society, the inevitable clash as the rising merchant classes struggled to wrest power from the old, feudal aristocracy. Others regard it as an essentially religious conflict, between on the one hand the forces of the Reformation – Protestants and Puritans – and on the other those of the Counter-Reformation, led by the Catholics. And there are those who see it as a sad but unavoidable product of the misrule of an incompetent monarch, Charles I.

But whatever its causes, the Civil War was to unleash forces and ideas the like of which had never been seen before. Many of these vanished again after the restoration of Charles II in 1660, but some survived to change our views of the world forever. John Bunyan was just one of many whose beliefs were forged in this bitter fight.

SCOTTISH COVENANTERS

If any one moment can be pointed to as triggering the Civil War, then it must be the day in February 1638 when hundreds of fiercely religious and independent Scots men and women gathered in Greyfriars Church in Edinburgh to sign a National Covenant pledging resistance to King Charles I's attempts to reform the church in Scotland. Such a momentous, and dangerous, step had been forced upon them, they argued, by the rash and high-handed attitude of the King and his religious mentor William Laud, Bishop of London.

At this time, Charles had ruled for almost a decade without Parliament – a period called the 'Personal Rule' – after he dissolved it in 1629, when he was refused finance for his wars abroad. Charles had always been a deeply religious, rather austere personality, and now he and Laud were trying to impose their own brand of Christianity on the Scots. It was the English Prayer Book which became the biggest bone of contention with

the Scots. The Scots, like many English people too, had long been disturbed by what they saw as Charles' papist tendencies – his French wife Henrietta Maria was an ardent Catholic – and this book was simply the last straw.

Later that year, the General Assembly of the Scottish Church annulled Charles' innovations, and, worse still, abolished bishops altogether. Charles decided there was no alternative but to enforce his will with military might. But the defiant Scots Covenanters quickly raised an army, and the King's preparations were so poor that the Covenanters were on the point of marching into England when a truce was agreed.

To deal with the crisis, Charles turned to the tough-minded Thomas Wentworth, Earl of Strafford, Lord Deputy of Ireland. He suggested recalling Parliament in order to vote taxes to pay for a better army. But the newly elected Parliament, after 11 years in the wilderness, was not prepared to

King and Queen
(below) Charles and his French queen presided over a fashionable court where dashing young poets with flowing hair dressed in rich satins. But beyond the closed court circle, the royal couple were deeply unpopular.

Cavalier attitudes
(right) The flamboyant supporters of King Charles I and the Church of England became known as Cavaliers. Contemptuously, they called their shorter-haired opponents 'Roundheads'.

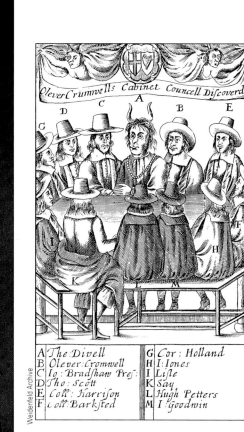

Clever Crumwells Cabinet Councell Difcovered

A	The Divell	G	Cor: Holland
B	Olever: Cromvell	H	I: Iones
C	Io: Bradshaw Pres:	I	Lisle
D	Tho: Scott	K	Say
E	Coll: Harrison	L	Hugh Petters
F	Coll: Barksted	M	I: Goodwin

War of words
Royalists and Parliamentarians opposed each other not only on the battlefield – floods of pamphlets represented the Parliamentarians as having a pact with the Devil (above), while the Royalists, in return, were accused of the most gruesome cruelties to women and children (below left).

Parliamentarian 'grandees'
Oliver Cromwell (below centre) emerged as a brilliant soldier and leader of men. His son-in-law Henry Ireton (below right) was his staunch supporter. Both tried to reach a settlement with the King but ultimately approved his execution.

meekly hand over the money; they wanted Charles to make amends for his negligence first.

Exasperated, Charles dissolved this 'Short' Parliament. But by this time, the Scots army had advanced as far south as Newcastle, and they agreed to stop only if they were paid £850 per day maintenance. Desperately short of money, Charles had to recall Parliament once more.

The House of Commons elected was full of men eager to make their mark, frustrated by so many years without a share in power, and also by the mishandling of the Scots crisis. From the start, under the skilled guidance of John Pym, it began to take steps against the King – or, rather, against the King's advisers, for faith in the monarchy was still too strong to countenance any suggestion that the King himself might be at fault.

The Long Parliament, as it came to be called, began by sending Strafford and Laud to the Tower, and followed this up with an act stating that no more than three years should ever pass again before Parliament was summoned. Soon, more extreme factions were demanding Strafford's head. Each day, the crowds that filled Whitehall grew bigger and more unruly, egged on by the more hot-headed MPs, and fear of these mobs soon tipped the balance in favour of the extremists. Parliament voted through the Act of Attainder that would claim Strafford's life, and in despair, Charles agreed.

It was escalating into a battle of wills between the King and his Parliament. Yet Charles, for all his obstinacy, was weak-willed, and too often in the past had seemed to resort to duplicity to win the day. Now few people trusted him.

The crisis might still have blown over had not terrible news reached Westminster in the summer of 1641 from over the Irish Sea. Made desperate by the English venom towards Catholics, the native Irish had risen in rebellion and bloodily slaughtered thousands, if not tens of thousands, of Protestant settlers. What was worse, the Irish insisted they were actually loyal subjects of the King, acting on his instructions – which he was rather too slow to deny.

Parliament expressed its outrage by passing a

New Model Army
After a number of indecisive battles, Oliver Cromwell suggested the formation of a 'New Model Army' (left) of professional soldiers, willing to move anywhere in the country with the course of war. The army was to be under impartial, non-political command. Sir Thomas Fairfax was commander-in-chief, and Cromwell (an exception to the non-political rule) as lieutenant-general led them into the Battle of Naseby.

Mary Evans Picture Library

Grand Remonstrance, roundly condemning the misrule of the last 15 years. Charles reacted by marching to the parliament-house at the head of a troop of 'cavaliers' bent on arresting five 'ringleaders'. But the five escaped, and Parliament, angered by this act of aggression, immediately demanded control of the army.

Unnerved by the turn of events, and the growing restlessness of the London mob, Charles withdrew with his retinue to York and there fired the opening salvoes in a protracted propaganda war, as each side tried to win hearts and minds with a flood of printed pamphlets, political tracts and satirical cartoons.

PROPAGANDA WAR

Charles projected himself as defender of the Church of England against Puritans and protector of time-honoured rights and privileges against radicals and the mob. The Parliamentarians, meanwhile, argued that they faced a King who was irresponsible, untrustworthy, and, in the hands of papist advisers, plotting to undermine the Protestant faith.

All through the winter of 1641-42 and the following spring, the war of words went on; both sides were trying to raise their own armies, and battling for possession of strategic towns.

There was a good deal of brinkmanship in this. Few people thought it would actually come to armed conflict. Perhaps Charles was still bluffing when he raised his standard at Nottingham on 22 August to rally all 'loyal Englishmen' to him. But the Parliamentarians had gone far too far to turn back now. The raising of the King's standard was the signal for war.

Three and a half centuries on, it is hard to discover what made one man fight for the King and another for Parliament. Indeed, perhaps few fought voluntarily at all, for 21 English counties spent the opening months of the war in a vain attempt to preserve their neutrality. And of those who did choose to fight, many simply followed their local magnate – or fought for the prospect of pay or plunder, since unemployment was at record levels.

Few of those who fought on either side had much military experience, and many were so plagued by doubts that they often held back from battle. Moreover, many commanders found their tactics dictated more by how willing their troops were to follow them than by military sense.

At first, the fortunes of war flowed in favour of the Royalists. The opening battle at Edgehill in Warwickshire, left both sides shaken, but the Royalists then marched towards London, and were only halted seven miles from the Houses of Parliament by a hastily gathered force of trained bands, apprentices and other volunteers. The following summer there were several victories in the southwest by the Royalist forces.

The Parliamentarians were thoroughly shaken, and it was only the success of a dramatic march to relieve Gloucester and the conclusion of an alliance with the Scots that revived their flagging spirits. The entry of the Scots into the war coincided with an upturn in Parliament's fortunes, for it was at this time that the army raised for Parliament in the prosperous and solidly Parliamentarian counties of East Anglia first made its mark. The commander of cavalry in this 'Eastern Association' army was the tough and ambitious MP for Cambridge, named Oliver Cromwell.

THE TURNING TIDE

When the Scots, the Eastern Association army and Parliament's northern army joined forces at Marston Moor near York on 2 July 1644, the Parliamentarians won their first major victory. Yet their very success sowed seeds of doubt in the minds of the Parliamentary commanders – aristocrats such as the Earls of Essex and Manchester – who saw in the prospect of a complete victory for Parliament the subversion of traditional values and the opening of the floodgates to radical ideas. So they hesitated and gave the Royalists time to recover. The war slipped into stalemate.

Impatient with their commanders, the more

Irish questions
Men and money were extracted from Ireland for the promise of religious tolerance. When the royal 'graces' were not forthcoming, the Catholic Irish rose and massacred thousands of Protestants. After Charles' death, Cromwell (above) crushed the rebellious Catholics.

Royal Oxford
After the battle of Edgehill in 1642, Charles marched into Oxford and this city became the Royalist headquarters. It was blockaded (left) before the Battle of Naseby, and besieged the following year, surrendering in June 1646 to the Parliamentarians. The King, however, had already slipped away.

Religious dissent
The Scots rebelled against Charles' high-handed attempts to bring the Church in Scotland into line with the Church of England. The introduction of the new Prayer Book led to riots in the churches (left) and to accusations of popery.

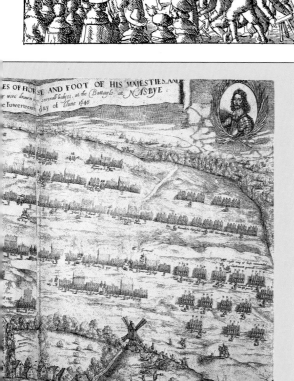

The Battle of Naseby
The Royalist forces suffered a crushing defeat at the hands of the New Model Army under the command of Fairfax and Cromwell in June 1645 (left). The Parliamentarian victory was so complete that the King even lost all his papers – and with them the last bit of political credibility.

radical members of Parliament led by Cromwell forced through a Self-Denying Ordinance, which required members of both Houses to give up their command – so that the army might be led by men with no political entanglements. Interestingly, Cromwell was the one exception to this rule. They also determined to create a 'New Model Army', made up of professional soldiers who would willingly serve anywhere in the country, to replace the ramshackle local troops who were racked by uncertain loyalties and desertions as soon as they ventured beyond their home territory.

The New Model Army took all winter to raise and train. But its entry into the war the next spring proved decisive. A series of minor triumphs in the south was followed by a crucial victory over the Royalists at Naseby in Northamptonshire. The Royalist forces were shattered. A year later, in 1646, Oxford, Charles' capital throughout the war, fell, and the Parliamentary forces marched into the city – only to find that Charles had already slipped away in disguise to give himself up to the Scots in Newark.

Now the fighting was over, the Parliamentarians were thrown into a turmoil of doubt about their next move. For almost a year, Parliament debated, and deputations went to the King to negotiate a settlement. But the King stubbornly refused any terms, still hoping for support from the Scots, or his Catholic friends abroad.

Into the vacuum poured a flood of radical ideas to solve the dilemma, both political, such as those of the Levellers, and religious, like those of the Ranters and Quakers. Such ideas had been in the air since before 1640, for the challenge to the authority of both the King and the bishops, represented by the Scots Covenant, had thrown into question the traditional hierarchy of society. If, as more extreme Puritans believed, salvation lay

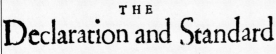

THE
Declaration and Standard

Of the *Levellers* of *England*;

Delivered in a Speech to his Excellency the Lord Gen. *Fairfax*, on *Friday* laft at White-Hall, by Mr. *Everard*, a late Member of the Army, and his Prophefie in reference thereunto; fhewing what will befall the Nobility and Gentry of this Nation, by their fubmitting to community; With their invitation and promife unto the people, and their proceedings in *Windfor* Park, *Oatlands* Park, and feverall other places; alfo, the Examination and confeffion of the faid Mr. *Everard* before his Excellency, the manner of his deportment with his Hat on, and his feverall fpeeches and expreffions, when he was commanded to put it off. Togyther with a Lift of the feverall Regiments of Horfe and Foot that have caft Lots to go for *Ireland*.

Imprinted at *London*, for *G. Laurenfon, April* 23. 1649.

The Levellers

A large number of political groups and religious sects emerged during the Civil War, among them the Levellers (left). They demanded a representative democracy – the abolition of monarchy, the right of all propertied men to vote and religious freedom. The Levellers were prominent in the Putney debates; only Cromwell and Ireton argued against their more radical demands.

Northamptonshire (he had been handed over by the Scots in 1647) and presented Parliament with a list of demands, claiming that they were doing so in the name of liberty and justice. Soon they presented their own solution to the problem, in the form of a new constitution.

The radical mood frightened the more conservative members of Parliament, who saw in it a threat to property. But when they tried to stage a counter-revolution by encouraging a violent mob to invade the House, the army moved in to take control. From now on, it was the army, not Parliament, who dictated the course of events. There followed a series of heated debates in Putney Church among army representatives about the form the constitution should take. Levellers were very much in the majority, arguing that the vote should be extended to all men of property, and Colonel Rainsborough declared that, 'The poorest he that is in England has a life to live as the greatest he, and therefore . . . every man that is to live under a government ought first by his own consent to put himself under that government.' Only Cromwell and his son-in-law, Henry Ireton, argued against them. But the debates were cut short by the news that Charles had escaped, come to terms with the Scots and persuaded them to send an army into England.

within each individual, not through the intercession of the Church, then the Church had no authority, and a labourer might find the correct road as well as any bishop.

No wonder, then, that the 1640s saw lay preachers attracting crowds of listeners in every town and village, while the priest often addressed a half-empty church. And as the war went on, a whole crop of radical religious sects, from Baptists (who so influenced John Bunyan) to Quakers, grew up, each finding its strength and ideas largely among ordinary people.

Just as the challenge to traditional authority opened the way for new religious beliefs, so they encouraged new political movements. If the Levellers argued only for reform of Church and Law and the extension of the vote to all men – or rather, all men of property – the Diggers or 'True Levellers' really did want to bring all society to the same level. The Diggers' mentor Gerard Winstanley argued that 'True freedom lies where a man receives his nourishment and preservation, and that is in the use of the earth.' They advocated a communist programme and began a communal cultivation of land at St George's Hill near London. As Parliament debated how to deal with the King, these movements reached their peak.

Meanwhile, the soldiers of the New Model Army were sitting around idly, yet had not received pay for 18 months – and were still in danger of being sued for damage to property during the war. When another summer came round and a settlement was no nearer, the soldiers decided to act, egged on by Leveller agitators. They kidnapped the King from Holmby House in

'Remember I am your King'

At the trial Charles I was accused of being a 'Tyrant, Traitor and Murderer, and a public and implacable Enemy to the Commonwealth of England'. Fifty-nine people signed his death warrant stating that he 'be put to death by the severing of his head from his body' (above).

The second Civil War was short, for Cromwell, now commander of the New Model Army, was resolute and vigorous, while the commanders of the Scottish army were not sure whether they ought to be fighting for Charles at all. The Scots' and Royalists' forlorn march south through Lancashire ended miserably when Cromwell's men fell upon them at Preston. Small Royalist rebellions in Kent and Essex were put down with equal speed.

The radicals were now certain that the only solution was to execute the King, and on 6 December 1648 Colonel Thomas Pride went to Parliament to remove or 'purge' those members likely to oppose this course of action. 'Pride's Purge' left about 70 members, who set up a High Court to try Charles. The trial was a formality, and on 30 January 1649 Charles went to his death.

HENRY FIELDING

1707-1754

For his commitment to combating hypocrisy and corruption –
both through his drama and in his newspapers and books –
Fielding was himself harassed by the Government. And while
he sought the lavish, flamboyant lifestyle of the country
gentleman and man-about-town, he could never escape his
creditors. This spirited, warm-hearted man loved life as much
as he hated crime in all its guises. These passions, tempered
with humour, permeate and enrich everything he wrote.

Law and Disorder

From a wild boy kicking against childhood injustices, Fielding grew into a man of reckless generosity and strong principles, pitting himself against crime, affectation and deception.

Nothing better illustrates the essence of Henry Fielding's character than the occasion when, having borrowed money to pay taxes due, he promptly bestowed the sum on a needier friend. To the waiting taxman, Fielding declared: 'Friendship has called for the money; let the collector call again.' Infinitely generous and deeply humane, he never prospered, yet made the world richer by his presence as well as his achievements as a writer, lawyer and journalist.

Henry Fielding was born at Sharpham Park near Glastonbury, the Somerset home of his maternal grandfather, on 22 April 1707. Henry's father Edmund was a spirited but hard-up army lieutenant who later rose to lieutenant-general. He was descended from William Feilding, the first Earl of

Denbigh; accounting for the different versions of the surname, Henry later joked that his branch of the family had been the first to master the art of spelling.

His mother, Sarah, was the eldest daughter of Sir Henry Gould, an eminent judge. Sarah and Edmund produced seven children – two boys and five girls – of whom Henry was the first. His brother and three of his sisters were born after the family moved to East Stour, Dorset, following grandfather Sir Henry's death in 1710; Sarah, born during that year, also became a successful novelist.

Henry inherited his father's aristocratic high spirits and relaxed attitude to money. From his mother, bred amidst prosperous rural gentry, came compassion and sensibility. She doted on the

Eton exile
Unhappy domestic circumstances dispatched Henry to Eton (above). It was a 'sentence' that proved beneficial.

Rural birthplace
Henry Fielding was born at Sharpham Park (above) near Glastonbury Tor (left) in Somerset, in the house of his grandfather. (He was to follow his grandfather into the legal profession.) Before he was three, the family moved on to East Stour in Dorset, to the house which Henry would subsequently inherit.

George Arnald: Glastonbury Abbey with the Tor beyond/Private Collection/Bridgeman Art Library

Mansell Collection

religious loyalties, responded like any grieving, angry child. His disruptive behaviour confirmed his father's decision to end tuition by private tutors and send him to a public (private) school.

Eton, unlike many other schools, was not a college where upper-class louts treated masters like servants, but a disciplined centre of excellence. It was the making of Henry, who recovered his affable equilibrium and became 'uncommonly versed in the Greek authors and an early master of the Latin classics'. His contemporaries included Thomas Arne, who later composed the music of *Rule Britannia!*, William Pitt the Elder and George Lyttelton (or Lyttleton); the latter two were friends of Henry's destined to become leading statesmen.

Canaletto: Eton College/National Gallery, London

Mary Evans Picture Library

Key Dates

1707 born near Glastonbury, Somerset

1718 mother dies

1719 sent to Eton

1725 attempts to abduct Sarah Andrew

1728 first play produced

1728-29 attends Leiden University

1734 marries Charlotte Cradock

1737 censorship laws end his playwriting

1739 starts *Champion* newspaper

1740 qualifies as barrister

1741 first novel, *Shamela*

1744 Charlotte dies

1745-46 runs *True Patriot* newspaper

1747 marries Mary Daniel

1748 appointed JP

1749 *Tom Jones*

1754 dies in Lisbon

warm-hearted, mischievous little boy 'so formed for happiness', as his cousin Lady Mary Wortley Montagu, a writer and society wit, said of him.

Yet Henry's secure foundations were shaken in 1718. His mother died, her health doubtless undermined by the rapid succession of childbirths. The next year his father married again. Henry's stepmother, Elizabeth, was an Italian widow who became instantly unpopular with her stepchildren and most of her other new relations. She was a Roman Catholic and the strongly Protestant Goulds were especially outraged at this.

Henry, whose writings would reflect their

Spectrum Colour Library

Dutch interlude
Like his fellow-writers James Boswell and Oliver Goldsmith, Fielding completed his studies in the picturesque town of Leiden (left), Holland.

Drury Lane première
Fielding's first play was mounted at the Theatre Royal, Drury Lane (above). It was a heartfelt comedy about disappointed love.

Henry's resentment of his stepmother did not extend to the six sons she bore his father, and he grew particularly fond of his half-brother John, who was blind, probably from birth. Henry, it seems, was liable to uncontrolled shows of emotion, and in 1725, soon after leaving Eton, he fell headlong in love with a girl at Lyme Regis and tried to abduct her one Sunday.

Sarah Andrew, a wealthy young heiress, was on her way to church at the time. Her guardian reported the incident, claiming he went in fear of the physically powerful youth, now grown to over six feet. Magistrates ordered Fielding to keep the peace.

Sarah was moved away to another guardian and married his son. Fielding's revenge was sweet – and creative; all his feelings as 'an injured lover' went into his first play. Freely adapted from a satire by the Latin poet Juvenal, the comedy *Love in Several Masques* was presented at the Theatre Royal in Drury Lane on 16 February 1728.

Its success, however, did not pay limitlessly for reckless enjoyment of London's pleasures. Fielding felt obliged to choose between 'the career of a hackney coachman and the career of a hackney writer'. With the sentimental comedies of late Restoration drama proving popular and profitable, a promising future beckoned – and Fielding strove for fortune as well as fame.

DRAMATIC ACHIEVEMENTS

His family decided he would be better equipped if he received further education, so Fielding was enrolled at Leiden University in the Netherlands – a fashionable and first-rate seat of learning. He worked very hard and greatly enlarged his knowledge of classical literature. After about 18 months he returned to England – apparently because his prodigal father could no longer afford the fees – and resumed his budding career as a playwright and author.

His energy was prodigious and he wrote at speed, turning out no less than 25 dramatic works between 1729 and 1737 – farces, light comedies, political satires and ballad operas. *The Author's Farce*, a parody of the pretensions Fielding detested, and *The Grub-Street Opera* bore resemblance to John Gay's brilliant *Beggar's Opera* of 1728. He was also influenced by the French farceur Molière, producing what is still considered the best, most original translation of his *L'Avare (The Miser)*. The hilarious burlesque *Tom Thumb* and the farce *Rape upon Rape*, revamped in the 1960s as the musical *Lock Up Your Daughters*, are the best-known survivors of Fielding's plays.

Fielding's reformist moral stance, so entertainingly clothed in his characters' exuberant, often licentious, conduct was already evident. Many critics regarded his work as coarse, and one of the most condemned plays was *The Modern Husband* (1732) which Fielding said was intended to make 'modern vice detestable'.

The Seventh Day.
For the Benefit of the AUTHOR.
By the Company of Comedians,
AT the New Theatre in the Hay-
market, To-morrow being Wednesday the 7th of April,
will be prefented, a New Play call'd,
The TRAGEDY of TRAGEDIES.
OR,
The Life and Death of Tom Thumb *the Great.*
To which will be added,
The AUTHOR's FARCE.
In which will be introduc'd an Operatical Puppet-fhow, call'd
The PLEASURES of the TOWN.
The Boxes not being equal to the great Demand of Places, (at the Defire of feveral Ladies of Quality) Pit and Boxes will be laid together, and none admitted into either but by printed Tickets, which will be deliver'd at the Theatre at 5 s. each, Gall. 2 s.
To prevent the Ladies waiting, none but the Gallery Doors will be open'd till Five o' Clock.
N. B. The New Opera call'd The WELCH OPERA, written by the Author of The TRAGEDY of TRAGEDIES, is deferr'd till Eafter Week.

Hogarth: The Four Times of Day – Morning/National Trust, Upton House, Oxfordshire/Bridgeman Art Library

Mutual respect
Fielding had a longstanding friendship with the artist William Hogarth, who illustrated one of his earliest plays. Fielding repaid the compliment by likening Bridget Allworthy in Tom Jones *to the central figure in Hogarth's painting (above).*

Tragedy of Tragedies
Fielding made his name by sending up the theatrical fashions of the time, as with the two productions billed left. But he could turn his hand to all manner of entertainment and was not averse to 'cashing in' on the taste for sentiment and vacuous comedy.

Fotomas

He dedicated the play to his cousin Lady Mary who took no offence and continued to offer affectionate encouragement. She was influential at court and her support was useful. Though a natural Whig (supporter of social reform), Fielding was not at first politically motivated; he nevertheless aligned himself with the 'court' party, the Tories, who were in opposition to the ruling Whigs and their leader, Sir Robert Walpole. It was to prove a fateful choice.

The charming young man-about-town was meanwhile spending as fast as he earned, pawning his velvet suit when short of cash. Fielding loved life and people, and was at ease with all levels of society in the teeming, squalid capital whose customs and habits both fascinated and repelled him in equal measure.

His outspokenness meant that Fielding was unpopular in certain circles, but he undoubtedly had a genius for friendship, one of his warmest relationships being with the great painter and engraver William Hogarth. Their long friendship began when Hogarth designed the frontispiece for the printed version of *Tom Thumb* (1730). At about the same time Fielding met and fell in love with his bride-to-be, Charlotte Cradock.

Clandestine marriage?

It is said that Henry eloped with Charlotte Cradock to marry secretly at St Mary's, Charlcombe, in Somerset (right). Her mother seems to have opposed the marriage, but must have relented later, for Charlotte received a substantial bequest.

Man at law

Pressing financial need probably forced Fielding to study law at the Middle Temple, London (left). While such a career meant wealth for some, Fielding drew small rewards and cast about for better, more congenial work – journalism and novel-writing.

Charlotte was a beautiful young woman living quietly with her mother and two sisters in Salisbury, Wiltshire. Sometime during 1734 the couple eloped – possibly because of opposition from the Cradock family – and were married. They went to live in East Stour at the house Fielding had inherited from his mother. They were blissfully happy, utterly devoted, and soon had a son. He died in infancy; but their grief was tempered with joy at the subsequent arrival of two daughters. Fielding was a doting parent.

He lived extravagantly, retaining servants in costly yellow livery, and entertaining regularly. But neighbouring squires disliked the convivial, champagne-loving 'Londoner' who poked gentle fun at their provincial ways. Early in 1736, Henry and Charlotte Fielding returned to the city. He had used up most of her £1500 dowry and was running short of money.

If 1735 had been an unproductive year – his sole work, *The Universal Gallant*, was an atypically dull comedy which flopped – 1736 saw a complete reversal. Fielding wrote the highly successful *Pasquin* and *Tumble-Down Dick*, presenting the

<hr />

Fact or Fiction

"COMFORT OF MY LIFE"

Fielding's adored first wife, Charlotte, died tragically young after 10 years of marriage. She is immortalized as Sophia in *Tom Jones* and as the heroine of *Amelia*. Both have her looks and "sweetness of disposition"; Amelia even has the broken nose Charlotte suffered in a coach accident.

The Bench

The plays Fielding wrote before he trained for the Law were scathing about the legal profession (above), which was then mercenary, nepotistic and open to corruption. Though Fielding cared deeply about justice, he himself owed his place on the Bench to the influence of an old friend.

plays himself at the New Theatre in London's Haymarket.

He followed in 1737 with one of his last plays, *The Historical Register*. Like the previous two, it was well-acclaimed and highly satirical – but more sharply-focused. Fielding's target in the mock auction of virtues that attract no bids was not just corrupt government in general, but Walpole in particular as "the fount of corruption" (his label in the press).

If the first minister was seeking an excuse to gag his increasingly vocal critics – and it has been suggested that he cunningly procured the play for

Urban resting place
Though she died in Bath, Charlotte was brought back for burial at St Martin-in-the-Fields, London (above). Fielding's grief 'approached to frenzy'.

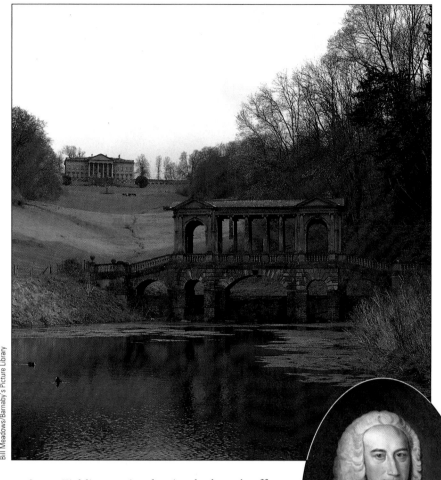

this purpose – he now had all the ammunition needed. Walpole introduced a restrictive bill, the second in two years. Against strong opposition, the Licensing Act gained royal assent on 21 June 1737. Through the Lord Chamberlain, the Government could and did censor; this power went unrepealed until 1968.

To more committed political satirists, the legislation meant disaster; to Fielding, whose intellectual horizons were unusually broad, it meant new challenges, new opportunities. He turned to journalism and law.

PART-TIME BARRISTER
On 1 November 1737 he entered the Middle Temple, qualifying as a barrister on 20 June 1740. Thereafter he joined the Western Circuit (of court sittings), but attracted few clients. During his unusually short period of intensive study, he continued writing and, with the American essayist James Ralph, produced a thrice-weekly newspaper, *The Champion,* a moderately successful imitation of Richard Steele's famous *Spectator.*

Fielding might have continued on the fringes of literature but for the appearance in November 1740 of Samuel Richardson's debut novel, *Pamela.* Amused, but irritated by its prudishness, Fielding dashed off a bawdy and cynical send-up *Shamela* (1741). Though published anonymously, it was identifiably his work. Richardson, cold and humourless, was so deeply offended that he never

spoke to Fielding again, despite the latter's efforts to make amends, and sneered at him publicly as 'this fashionable author'.

The similarly mocking yet more successful *Joseph Andrews,* influenced by the Spanish writer Cervantes, was published in 1742 – also anonymously – and sold 6500 copies. It earned Fielding a much-needed £183 as well as some claim to treatment as a serious novelist.

In the same year Fielding published *Jonathan Wild.* An ironic glorification of the self-styled 'Thief-Taker General', it comprised a damning indictment of the corrupt system that had allowed a vicious criminal to organize robberies and then receive rewards for restoring the stolen goods. It signalled Fielding's growing preoccupation with legal affairs, but personal matters prevailed for the next few years. Charlotte, heart-sick over the death of their youngest daughter in 1742, and harassed incessantly by debt-collectors, fell ill the following year. Fielding took her for treatment to Bath, where she died in his arms of fever in 1744.

FRENZIED ACTIVITY
Near-demented with grief, Fielding flung himself into his work, engaging in pro-government journalism (Walpole had been ousted in February 1742) and almost single-handedly running two papers in succession, *The True Patriot,* and then *The Jacobite's Journal.* The latter was launched eight days after he remarried on 27 November

Country retreat
Sued and harried by creditors in London, Fielding found more peace in Bath, where he made friends with a local businessman, Ralph Allen (above). Allen drew around him a circle of artistic men, including the poet Alexander Pope. Allen's great affluence, combined with good taste, expressed itself in his home, Prior Park (top). Allen supplied Fielding with the inspiration for a fictional 'hero' – and with money.

1747. His bride, Mary Daniel, a Londoner and Charlotte's faithful former maid, was six months pregnant at the time. Fielding's spiteful, supercilious enemies were jubilant.

However, Fielding's detractors obstructed neither the couple's happiness – their union was blessed with two sons and three daughters – nor his appointment as a Justice of the Peace for Westminster in December 1748 and, soon after, for Middlesex as well (he owed the preferment to his old schoolfriend Lyttelton).

DR JOHNSON'S BLOCKHEAD

Fielding's house and court were in London's Bow Street, where he is remembered as a wise and kind 'beak', an outspoken opponent of extortionate 'trading justices', and an energetic upholder of law-and-order. Following his unanimous election as chairman of Westminster Quarter Sessions in 1749, he worked with his half-brother Sir John – by now his assisting magistrate – on plans that led to the smashing of gangs of robbers and highwaymen through the use of paid informers.

Fielding's masterpiece *Tom Jones* was published in February the same year and, though condemned as 'vicious' by Dr Johnson (a Richardson fan, he thought Henry 'a blockhead'), it sold 10,000 copies in nine months, was in great demand abroad, and netted the author a princely £700.

The enormously long novel was written from about 1747 onwards, some of it at Bath, where Fielding was a frequent guest at the Palladian mansion of his friend and 'munificent patron' Ralph Allen. A rich local businessman and philanthropist, Allen re-emerged in the book as the laudable Squire Allworthy, his home as Paradise Hall.

Fielding's last great work of fiction was *Amelia* (1749), the first English novel of social protest. It

HOGARTH

London-born William Hogarth (1697-1764) was one of the era's most celebrated artists. He was still relatively unknown when he met Fielding in 1730, but gained overnight fame three years later with a set of six engravings called *A Harlot's Progress*. This and its many successors – *A Rake's Progress, Gin Lane* and *Industry and Idleness* – satirized social evils with power and caustic humour, using line to much the same effect as his friend Fielding used his pen.

Hogarth: The Painter and his Pug/Tate Gallery, London

Last days in Portugal
An ailing Fielding took rooms in Lisbon (below), and lived on a pound a week. His footman ran off, stealing money; the lovesick maid followed the ship's captain back to England; and his wife Mary fell ill. Henry died in October and was buried among expatriate English wine-merchants. Ralph Allen supported his surviving family.

was less good-humoured than *Tom Jones*, though his publisher, Andrew Millar, reputedly paid £1000 for the copyright.

Exhausted and desperately ill with gout, an acutely painful arthritic disease, Fielding resigned from the Bench in April 1754. Hobbling on crutches, he sailed for Lisbon two months later, accompanied by his wife and his surviving daughter from his first marriage.

Complaining crustily that the Portuguese capital was 'the nastiest city in the world', Fielding remained otherwise cheerful, but despite the warm climate he never regained good health. He was released from suffering on 8 October 1754 and was buried in the city's English cemetery.

Mary Evans Picture Library

TOM JONES

In this lusty attack on hypocrisy, Fielding's disarming hero cavorts his way through countless escapades, both tortuous and amorous.

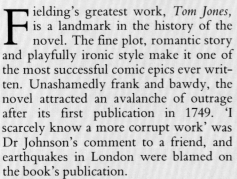

George Stubbs: Mother and Child/Tate Gallery, London

the schoolmaster Partridge, is accused of being the mother and duly banished from the parish. Later Partridge is also implicated and although he fervently denies paternity, he too is forced to leave. Another child joins Tom in the nursery – the son of Allworthy's sister Bridget and her unpleasant husband Captain Blifil. Master Blifil is the legitimate heir to Allworthy's estate, and is treated more favourably than the illegitimate Tom by most of the household, especially the tutors Thwackum and Square. Generous, impetuous and headstrong, Tom is quite different from the hypocritically pious Blifil and remains Allworthy's favourite.

When he reaches maturity, Tom begins an affair with Molly Seagrim, Black George the gamekeeper's daughter. She

F ielding's greatest work, *Tom Jones,* is a landmark in the history of the novel. The fine plot, romantic story and playfully ironic style make it one of the most successful comic epics ever written. Unashamedly frank and bawdy, the novel attracted an avalanche of outrage after its first publication in 1749. 'I scarcely know a more corrupt work' was Dr Johnson's comment to a friend, and earthquakes in London were blamed on the book's publication.

Nowadays such reactions seem unbelievable, for the amorous adventures of Tom Jones are wonderfully entertaining and firmly set in a moral context. And in best storytelling tradition, in the end, good triumphs over evil.

GUIDE TO THE PLOT

Squire Allworthy, a wealthy, amiable widower, returns to his home, Paradise Hall in Somerset, after several months' absence to find a baby asleep in his bed. Captivated by its innocence, he decides to bring the baby up as his own and names him Tom Jones. Jenny Jones, servant of

David Wilkie: Man and Horse/Victoria and Albert Museum, London/Bridgeman Art Library

Surprise package
When Squire Allworthy finds a baby (above left) between his sheets, he is transfixed by "the beauty of innocence" and determines to bring him up as his own.

Churchyard battle
Pregnant Molly (above) makes an unwise appearance at church and inspires "the fury of the women". Undaunted, she takes them on single-handed, until Tom comes to her aid.

A selfless gesture
Distraught at the plight of the gamekeeper's family, Tom sells his horse (left) at a neighbouring fair and passes the proceeds on to 'Black George'.

there by her in anger, he is mortified and sets off immediately to look for her.

Eventually they all make their way to London. Tom and Partridge stay in lodgings; Sophia seeks shelter with her relative Lady Bellaston, who is smitten by Tom. The plot thickens. A Lord Fellamar, who wants Sophia for himself, arranges for a press-gang to spirit Tom off to sea. Tom ends up in prison for defending himself against attack by a mistakenly jealous Irishman.

The hero is now at his lowest ebb, but the arrival of Squire Allworthy marks a change in his fortunes. Past deceits and hypocrisy are exposed, Tom's true parentage is revealed and Fielding allows "the beauty of virtue" finally to prevail.

A MOCK-HEROIC TALE

Tom Jones is a rambling tale of adventure and intrigue in which the plot has priority over character. It is a huge and minutely structured novel with exactly 200 chapters. The rapid changes of scene and vast array of minor characters are essential to the lively comic style of the novel.

In spite of the intricacy and complexity of the story, it flows easily from one character's actions to another's, and is interspersed with Fielding's comments to his readers. In his dedication Fielding explains, "I have employed all the wit and humour of which I am master in the following history; wherein I have

A perilous ride
Sophia's morning outing (above) has mixed consequences – thrown from her "unruly beast", Sophia suddenly finds herself saved by Tom, but this pleasant surprise palls when she learns that Tom has broken his arm.

Love in the bushes
Pledging himself to Sophia in his thoughts – heart and soul – Tom unexpectedly happens upon the wayward Molly Seagrim (below). He promptly retires to "the thickest part of the grove" to rekindle a flame.

becomes pregnant and Tom promises to stay by her, but finds himself falling in love with the beautiful Sophia Western. Sophia's father, the bumptious Squire Western, greatly enjoys Tom's company but is nonetheless outraged when he discovers his daughter's feelings for Tom. Tom's illegitimacy places him completely out of reach of the nobly born Sophia, and he leaves his benefactor's house to make his own way in the world.

Squire Western then decides to ensure Sophia gives up Tom by arranging a marriage between her and the hateful Blifil. Unable to bear the idea, she runs away, hoping to track down Tom. Tom, meanwhile, is travelling with Partridge, now a barber surgeon, who becomes his devoted if loose-tongued servant. One of Tom's many adventures involves rescuing a distressed, half-naked Mrs Waters from the hands of a murderous Army officer. Tom spends the night with her at an inn not knowing that his beloved Sophia is under the same roof. When Tom finds Sophia's muff in his bedroom in the morning, left

> "... Jones probably thought one woman better than none, and Molly as probably imagined two men to be better than one."

endeavoured to laugh mankind out of their favourite follies and vices."

For all its irony and comic absurdity, *Tom Jones* is nonetheless a very moral novel. Without being pompous, Fielding reminds us that generosity of action is worth far more than generosity of spirit. Tom reflects that "the delight of giving happiness to others . . . [is] a sweeter pleasure, than the ambitious, the avaricious, or the voluptuous man can ever obtain." Most of the characters in the novel divide sharply into 'good' and 'bad', often appearing simply in order to make Fielding's point more forcibly.

EXPOSING HYPOCRISY

The sadistic, hypocritical Thwackum and the artful, opportunistic Square are clear examples of moral types. Their function in the novel is essentially to highlight the duplicity so despised by Fielding. His professed Christianity makes Thwackum's blind selfishness all the more sinful. His frantic attempts to impress Squire Allworthy by expounding at great length on philosophical and religious points are despicable, and fail repeatedly.

Tom is the most interesting of the 'good' characters. For all his youthful folly, poor judgement and energetic sexuality, "the beauty of innocence" which he exuded as a tiny baby never quite leaves him. His openness of spirit and capacity to think well of others lead him into all manner of difficulties, but it is these very qualities – his benevolence and integrity – which save him in the end.

In his treatment of sexual behaviour, Fielding attempts to broaden the moral perspective of his day. He reveals that indignation at promiscuity is not necessarily a virtuous or indeed an honest stance. Even marital intentions are suspect, often prompted by greed. Captain Blifil's designs to marry Bridget "were strictly honourable as the phrase is, that is to rob a lady of her fortune by marriage". Tom is far from chaste, but hopes that he has never hurt any woman, and declares, "nor would I, to procure pleasure to myself, be knowingly the cause of misery to any human being."

Tom's sexual appetite is portrayed as both normal and healthy. Allworthy himself, we are told, enjoyed his share of youthful affairs. And Squire Western, an essentially good man, quite relishes the thought of Tom's sexuality – and even that of his daughter, once her marriage has been decided. This lusty warmth is shown as infinitely preferable to Blifil's cold, calculated self-interest.

Chief among the targets for Fielding's

Unjustly confined
(left) Imprisoned for his part in a duel, Tom suffers doubly – for having shed a man's blood and for jeopardizing the love of Sophia.

Tavern politics
Meeting some British redcoats at an inn (above), Tom volunteers. He supports George II against Scotland's 'Young Pretender'.

Mary Evans Picture Library

"Fortune will never have done with me, 'till she hath driven me to distraction. But why do I blame Fortune? . . . All the dreadful mischiefs which have befallen me, are the consequences only of my own folly and vice."

FOUNDLING HOSPITAL

In 1739 a merchant sailor, Captain Thomas Coram (right), established the London Foundling Hospital in response to the plight of babies he saw abandoned near his Rotherhithe home. Among those who helped raise money were the artist William Hogarth and the composer Handel who donated the manuscript of his *Messiah* to the hospital.

Initially, the policy of the hospital was to accept any baby left at its doors, but this soon proved unmanageable. It is claimed that of 15,000 children left there during a four-year period, 10,000 died. Tragically, after such impressive beginnings, the Hospital became known as a 'charnel house for the dead'.

Fotomas

William Sharpe: The Billet/Fine Art Photographic Library

sionally bemoans his fate, but he does not try to overturn it. The implication is that one's birthright does actually matter. Mrs Miller's attempt to comfort Tom, though a cogent sociological argument, is of little use: "the words 'dishonourable birth' are nonsense . . . unless the word 'dishonourable' be applied to the parents; for the children can derive no real dishonour from an act of which they are entirely innocent." But for Tom, it is the fact of his illegitimacy which determines his future. The ultimate goal of the novel is to bring the lovers together without threatening the basis of social order. The tacit assumption is that it would be unthinkable for a bastard to marry gentry.

Angiolo Romagnoli: Bringing the Message/Fine Art Photographic Library

Secret letters
Unable to see her, Tom continues his suit of Sophia by letter. But her maidservant Betty (above left) proves less loyal than she might be . . .

A happy ending?
(below) Eventually, after countless turns of fortune, Tom is proved worthy of Sophia – but how can he overcome the barriers of class?

Heywood Hardy: The Squire's Visit (detail)/Fine Art Photographic Library

pen is hypocrisy, which he detests in any shape or form, calling it "the bane of all virtue, morality, and goodness". This contrast between appearance and reality forms a major theme running through the novel. Blifil, Bridget, Allworthy, Thwackum, Square, the Seagrim family, many of the servants and the London aristocracy all pretend to be something they are not. Fielding speaks directly on the subject in Chapter Four ('a necessary apology for the author') of Book Three: "A treacherous friend is the most dangerous enemy . . . both religion and virtue have received more real discredit from hypocrites, than the wittiest profligates or infidels could ever cast upon them."

The most "treacherous friend" in the novel is young Blifil, whose malicious treatment of Tom is all the more despic-

able for his pretensions to virtue and piety. "One of the best-natured gentlemen in the universe", Tom himself is never guilty of hypocrisy. His openness and truthfulness are his passport to virtue.

Another object of Fielding's wrath is the decadence of society lords and ladies, and again he uses his pen to prick their hypocrisy and to reveal the corruption and viciousness of their treatment of human life. But in spite of satirizing the upper classes, the novel upholds the notion of social class divisions as being right and proper. For all the ups and downs of Tom's adventures, the whole momentum of the plot is towards re-establishing the norm found in Squire Allworthy's Paradise Hall.

Tom never questions the fact that he cannot marry Sophia Western. He occa-

CHARACTERS IN FOCUS

The huge cast of characters in *Tom Jones* divides loosely into those central to the plot and those central to Fielding's moral purpose. Although the main figures span both categories, the minor ones tend to represent types rather than real people. Their names – Allworthy, Square, Thwackum – give an idea of their character, social class and their function in the novel.

WHO'S WHO

Tom Jones The hero of the tale who survives his turbulent fortunes with charm and decency.

Squire Allworthy Famed for his "benevolent heart", he is unfailingly generous and 'worthy'.

Bridget Allworthy Allworthy's sister, who hides a secret behind her mask of respectability.

Sophia Western Her "beauty, fortunes, sense, and amiable carriage" totally captivate the youthful Tom.

Squire Western Affectionate and fun-loving although given to terrible rages, Sophia's father embodies the best and the worst traits of a country squire.

Blifil Allworthy's unctuous nephew and heir. Intensely jealous of Tom, he is dangerous in his malice.

Partridge "A very good-natured fellow" though somewhat cowardly, he is powerfully bound to Tom.

Mrs Waters "Of the middle age", and not renowned for her beauty, she is an intriguing figure with whom Tom enjoys a night of passion.

Thwackum "Proud and ill-natured", he makes Tom's life a misery in the school-room.

Molly Seagrim Tom's first amorous dalliance, she is sensuously appealing.

Black George Molly's father, the gamekeeper, who "was, in the main, a peaceable kind of fellow" if somewhat greedy.

Heywood Hardy: A Meeting by the Stile (detail)/Christie's, London/Bridgeman Art Library

Always open and generous, Tom Jones (left) "was in reality one of the handsomest young fellows in the world. His face, besides being the picture of health, had in it the most apparent marks of sweetness and good-nature." Although certainly not virtuous in the conventional sense – apt to tumble too easily in and out of women's beds – he is nonetheless the embodiment of decency and honour. He sells his prized possessions in order to give money to Black George the gamekeeper, he stands by Molly Seagrim whom he mistakenly believes he has wronged, and he repeatedly rescues damsels in distress. He is impetuous – "a giddy youth" – but lovable; tough, humorous, lusty and, ultimately, very moral. An "inoffensive lad amidst all his roguery", though "somewhat passionate", he is, in Partridge's words, "one of the best-natured gentlemen in the universe". Fielding, it would seem, valued good nature above all.

Wright of Derby: Portrait of a Gentleman (detail)/Private Collection/Bridgeman Art Library

"A favourite of both Nature and Fortune", Mr Allworthy (right) is, as his name suggests, a solid, worthy gentleman. From Nature "he derived an agreeable person, a sound constitution, a solid understanding, and a benevolent heart." From Fortune he gained "the inheritance of one of the largest estates in the country". His worthiness, however, is occasionally marred by his judgement. He gladly welcomes the foundling Tom Jones into his heart, in spite of the baby's apparent illegitimacy, but wrongly rejects others, and later even Tom, and is too easily duped by the devious Captain Blifil, Thwackum and Square. When the truth comes to light, however, he is quick to make amends.

Hogarth: William Jones (detail)/Private Collection/Bridgeman Art Library

Eighteen-year-old Sophia Western (right) is the heroine of the piece – beautiful, nobly born and pure. "Her shape was not only exact, but extremely delicate; and . . . her mind was every way equal to her person." She falls passionately in love with Tom and remains true to him in spite of the differences in their backgrounds, taking on her father's outrage as well as society's snobbish displeasure. Spirited and determined, she chooses to run away from home rather than be forced to marry the hateful Blifil. "To say the truth, it was very difficult for anyone to know that young lady without loving her", Fielding remarks. Tom for his part certainly loves her, although deeming himself undeserving of her affection – "her thoughts of me I shall never be worthy of", he cries at one point, "she is all gentleness, kindness, goodness."

Threading his way through the tapestry of the novel, Partridge (below) "was one of the best-natured fellows in the world" and "reputed the wit of the country". Originally a schoolmaster, his fortunes take a turn for the worse when he is thought guilty of having fathered Tom with his servant Jenny Jones. He is banished, to reappear as an itinerant barber and become Tom's loyal companion and manservant on his adventures. Partridge plays a comic role throughout, continually getting into scrapes and bursting into Latin at the slightest opportunity, but he is essentially a decent and charming fellow, convinced that "too much learning" has been his downfall.

Sir Joshua Reynolds: Lady Worsley/by kind permission of the Earl of Harewood/Royal Academy of Arts

licious, hypocritical
, Blifil (above) is
ful heir to the
orthy estate. Brought
ith Tom, Blifil devotes
onsiderable energies to
ning him and
rmining his uncle's
tion for him. Physically
and spiritually
pt, he is the antithesis
m – "Master Blifil fell
short of his companion
amiable quality of
y". But more
icantly he is evil – a
ning, villainous,
olent liar.

Walter Dendy Sadler: Chance Companions (detail)/Fine Art Photographic Library

One of the more intriguing characters, Mrs Waters (below) has "a very uncommon share of understanding". She appears first "stript half naked, under the hands of a ruffian", and soon is seen similarly exposed only this time more pleasurably in the company of Tom. Believed at a certain point to be his mother, she alone knows the truth about his parentage and ultimately unravels the remaining mysteries of the novel.

Boucher: Half-naked Woman Bending Over/Musee des Beaux-Arts, Lille

FATHER OF THE NOVEL

Initially a playwright, Fielding perfected his literary talents only after he turned to fiction. Making use of his own wild experiences, he created a new genre: 'the comic epic in prose'.

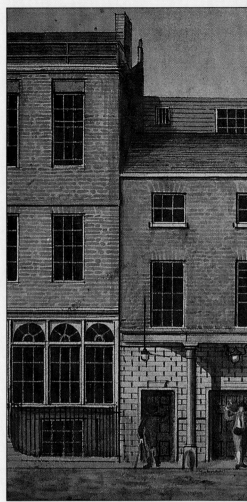

The novels of Henry Fielding have never lost favour with the public, or with fellow writers as different in outlook as Sir Walter Scott, Charles Dickens and Somerset Maugham. Fielding's easy conversational style, infectious high spirits, common-sense attitudes and seemingly effortless flow of humorous invention have given his fiction a universal appeal.

His writing has also created an impression of spontaneity and carefreeness which is reinforced by what we know of his reckless, improvident life-style. One of the few descriptions we have of Fielding at work portrays him 'meditating for the good and entertainment of the public, with my two little children (as is my usual course to suffer them) playing near me'. It is easy to think of a man working in such circumstances as a 'natural' writer rather than a dedicated professional.

Fielding's first literary career seems to fit in with this picture. By his own account he had to choose between becoming a hackney coachman and a hackney writer, and therefore set up as a dramatist. An actor friend, Arthur Murphy, has recorded that Fielding devised many scenes after returning late from a tavern, writing on the left-over wrappings of the tobacco he used so liberally.

Nevertheless, Fielding was extremely successful in the theatre, writing more than 20 domestic comedies, farces and adaptations. For 100 years or more, his best known work was *The Life and Death of Tom Thumb the Great* (1730). This devastating parody of overblown tragedies became dated only when the kind of drama that inspired it had ceased to be familiar.

RUIN AND RESCUE

Fielding was particularly effective in making satirical points within a framework of farce, and *Pasquin* (1736), which sent up corrupt electioneering, had a box-office success that seemed likely to assure the author's future. But another Fielding play, *The Historical Register for the Year 1736*, brought the wrath of Sir Robert Walpole's government down on the theatre. His career as a playwright was ruined – or, to put it another way, he was saved for the novel.

Fielding was a talented popular playwright, but not a great one. In this field he seems never to have exerted his full powers, and he later remarked that he had left off writing for the stage at the point where he ought to have begun. However, he brought a gift for vivid dialogue over into the fiction which he began to produce a few years after he had quit the theatre.

Fielding was unusual in that he developed his distinctive manner in violent reaction against another writer's work. In 1740 a master printer, Samuel Richardson, published the immensely popular – and immensely long – *Pamela*.

George Lyttelton
'Best man' at Fielding's second wedding, Lyttelton (left) gave both moral and financial support during the writing of Tom Jones, *and helped Fielding become a magistrate.*

Mansell Collection

Woman of influence
Fielding's second cousin, Lady Mary Wortley Montagu (right), was an intelligent woman of great artistic taste. She eased his entry to the theatre world.

Victoria and Albert Museum, London/E.T. Archive

The SEVENTH DAY.
By the Company of Comedians, Hay-
market. To-morrow being Friday the 19th Day of July,
AT the New Theatre in the Hay-
will be presented, a new Comedy, call'd
RAPE upon RAPE:
OR,
The JUSTICE caught in his own TRAP.
Written by the Author of TOM THUMB.
With new Scenes and other Decorations.
To which will be added a New Tragedy, of one Act (never acted
but once) called
JACK the GIANT-KILLER.

Man of the theatre
*First resident
playwright, then
manager, director
and artistic controller,
Fielding oversaw the
staging of such plays
as his* Rape upon
Rape *(above) at the
Little (New)
Theatre (left).*

Parodying piety
*His contempt for the
cliché-ridden best-
seller* Pamela
*(illustrated below)
incited Fielding to
write first* Shamela
and then Joseph
Andrews.

These form most of the novel's content.

Most commentators have believed that Fielding started with the intention of writing a parody and was carried away by his own creative imagination. However, this is by no means certain, in view of the careful dovetailing of the plot elements from start to finish. In any event, *Joseph Andrews* is vintage Fielding and includes the character widely considered to be his finest single creation – the good, learned, unworldly, forgetful, utterly endearing Parson Abraham Adams.

CAREFUL PLOTTING

Joseph Andrews and the even greater *Tom Jones* (1749) represent the summit of Fielding's achievement. They also suggest that the picture of him as a 'natural', spontaneous writer is overdrawn. Whatever the origins of *Joseph Andrews*, it was carefully revised by Fielding in subsequent editions. Even more than the earlier book, *Tom Jones* has a plot that fulfilled Fielding's own requirement – that every incident should have a bearing on the rest, although the reader may not be aware of the fact until the end of the book. The measure of Fielding's success is that Samuel Taylor Coleridge considered that *Tom Jones* had one of the three best plots ever devised. Finally, *Tom Jones* was not dashed off: in his dedication to his friend George Lyttelton, Fielding implies just

This novel was presented as a series of letters, most of them supposedly written by a servant girl, Pamela Andrews, while she was being pursued by her young master, 'Mr B.' Intent upon seduction, he subjects Pamela to various perils (kidnapping, drugs, etc), but fails to conquer her virtue, and at last marries her.

Pamela evidently put Fielding entirely out of all patience, for he hit out at it on two separate occasions. In 1741 he published a parody of it, pointedly brief by contrast with Richardson's novel. *Shamela* purported to give the 'true' facts of the case – that Pamela (real name Shamela) was far from virtuous, but pretended to be so in order to gull Mr B. (real name Mr Booby), whom she betrayed both before and after their marriage.

In his first novel, *Joseph Andrews* (1742), Fielding attacked *Pamela* from a different angle. Joseph is Pamela's brother and, equally virtuous, he resists the attempts of Lady Booby to seduce him – the reversal of sexes making the entire episode ridiculous to 18th-century eyes. But then the story veers away from the *Pamela* pattern, as Joseph is turned out and undergoes a long series of adventures on the road.

the opposite, writing 'I here present you with the labour of some years of my life.'

Fielding was a highly original writer whose contribution to the English novel can hardly be overvalued. He was the first English writer of fiction to deal with every level of society from the aristocrat to the pickpocket or chambermaid; in this he was equalled only by Chaucer and Shakespeare among his predecessors. And he was the first English novelist to break away from the 'documentary' convention which made writers such as Defoe and Richardson present their stories as reports of real events, buttressed by laborious 'realistic' details and supposedly authentic documents and source material.

FACTLESS FICTION

Fielding mocked the convention in *Shamela* by treating Richardson's plot as a real event that could be reinterpreted if new 'documents' came to light. And in an entertaining fragment, *A Journey from This World to the Next* (1743), the narrative occurs in a manifestly absurd manuscript which becomes all the more ridiculous by being adorned with fatuous 'scholarly' footnotes. 'I profess fiction only', Fielding roundly declared in the preface to his *Miscellanies*, and in the major novels his interpolated essays and authorial remarks constantly remind us that we are reading fiction – and never more so than in the passages where Fielding pretends to follow the 'documentary' convention, solemnly assuring the reader that he has been unable

to find out whether a character sneezed four or five times.

Fielding was also 'the founder of a new province of writing', the comic epic, although he admitted a large debt to the Spanish classic *Don Quixote*, about the deluded 'Knight of the Doleful Countenance' who wandered the country sustaining humiliations instead of performing feats of valour. The title-page of *Joseph Andrews* carries a typically generous tribute: the book is said to be 'written in imitation of the manner of Cervantes, author of *Don Quixote*'.

Fielding aimed 'to describe human nature as it is, not as we would wish it to be'. Moreover 'I describe not men, but manners; not an individual, but a species'. It is a human nature whose less attractive traits are distanced by comedy, but Fielding held that episodes such as Nero ripping up his mother's belly (his own example) were beyond the range of the comic epic. Just as he ensured that his fiction should not be confused with reality, so he insisted that art and life were essentially separate. The basic subject of the comic epic, as Fielding defined it, is 'the Ridiculous', not 'great vices'.

A MODEST OBJECTIVE

There is a reforming impulse behind Fielding's writing, but his objective is modest: that 'thousands in their closets' should 'contemplate their deformity and endeavour to reduce it'. His morality places a high value on generosity of spirit

Tom Thumb
Jonathan Swift declared that he had laughed only twice in his life – once was at a performance of Fielding's mock-heroic stage farce, The Life and Death of Tom Thumb the Great (left).

Ruling party
(right) Sir Robert Walpole's government was rife with nepotism, but he was liked by both George II and Queen Caroline. Fielding's satire was powerless against him, whereas Walpole (seen left), successfully ended Fielding's theatrical career.

Mansell Collection

Hogarth and Thornhill: House of Commons in 1730/National Trust Photographic Library/Hawkley Studios

Joseph Andrews
This two-volume book (illustrated left) was written in nine months, published anonymously and sold 6500 copies in a year. Renowned for its characterization, it netted £183 11s.

Charlotte Charke
Fielding lured the daughter (right) of theatrical giant Colley Cibber to his own theatre company. A wild transvestite, she played male roles and helped Fielding lampoon her father.

Low life
Fielding used his fourth newspaper, The Covent Garden Journal, to focus on social evils (below). He also advertised in it for victims of crime and witnesses to come forward, to stop acquittals through lack of evidence.

(1752), which, because of its more sentimental tone has never been rated as highly by critics as *Joseph Andrews* and *Tom Jones*. At the time, however, *Amelia* sold better than any of Fielding's previous books.

Fielding's last book, *A Voyage to Lisbon* (1755), is chiefly of interest as an indirect self-portrait of the author. Mortally ill, he endures pain stoically. He continues to become indignant when confronted with brutality and corruption. And to the last he displays an unconquerable zest for life – a zest which is perhaps the ultimate reason for the enduring appeal of his greatest novels.

and a fundamental, untouchable innocence, so that it is doubtful whether he would really prefer to see Tom Jones perfectly chaste or Abraham Adams worldly wise. In fact another aspect of Fielding's originality is that his characters are not good or bad all the way through; and the reader is warned 'not to condemn a character as a bad one because it is not perfectly a good one'.

Fielding's abhorrence of contemporary abuses appears particularly strong in his other two novels. *Jonathan Wild* (1743) is a short, relentlessly ironic satire on the 'greatness' that can be achieved by the most ruthlessly self-seeking criminal in a world of criminals. Although Wild was a real fence and thief-taker, hanged in 1725, Fielding's satire was obviously intended to apply with equal force to the corrupt politicians of his day, notably Sir Robert Walpole, whose 20 years in political power had just ended when the novel was published. Vile prison conditions and ignorant, venal magistrates were among Fielding's targets in his last novel, *Amelia*

In his twenties Fielding was a prolific playwright with a talent for burlesque and satire. But when he flung one too many gibes at Sir Robert Walpole and the Whig Government, they effectively drove Fielding off the stage.

Ever the satirist, Fielding used his talents to send up Samuel Richardson's epic novel, *Pamela*. Fielding's parody, entitled *An*

Apology for the Life of Mrs Shamela Andrews, led to another novel, *Joseph Andrews* (1742), which brought a new vitality and sense of social reality to English fiction.

Fielding's *Miscellanies* (1743) included two contrasting works: *A Journey from This World to the*

Next, mixing fantasy with shrewd comments on human affairs, and an unflinching account of crime and low-life, *Jonathan Wild*. There followed his masterpiece, *Tom Jones* (1749), and the more sentimental *Amelia* (1752).

The stoical account of his final, futile search for health in *The Journal of a Voyage to Lisbon* was posthumously published in 1755.

JOSEPH ANDREWS

◆1742◆

Joseph Andrews begins his career as a stable lad (right) in the service of the Booby family. He is with the Boobys in London when Sir Thomas dies, and Lady Booby, who has long looked favourably on the handsome Joseph, makes advances to him. He, however, indignantly spurns her. As a result of this upright behaviour he is dismissed and decides to set out for his West Country home.

On the way he meets the learned, naïve, absent-minded curate of his village, Parson Abraham Adams, who discovers that he has forgotten to bring the sermons he intended to have printed in London. He joins Joseph and heads back with him. On their travels the two men rescue a young woman from the hands of some ruffians and discover that she is Fanny, the girl Joseph loves, who had come looking for him. The little party meet with many adventures until they are sheltered by Mr Wilson, a quiet country gentleman whose tale of a lost son has unexpected consequences for all of them.

George Morland: Horses in a Stable/Victoria and Albert Museum, London/Bridgeman Art Library

A JOURNEY FROM THIS WORLD TO THE NEXT

◆1743◆

Soon after death, the narrator is taken on an extraordinary conducted tour (left). In a celestial stagecoach, he and other passengers visit the City of Diseases, the Palace of Death, then lastly Elysium. Some may enter, while those not virtuous enough are sent back into the world to start again. A meeting with one who has been back a dozen times proves highly educational.

JONATHAN WILD

◆1743◆

Wild has all the qualities needed to succeed in crime – or politics (right). Starting out as a pickpocket, he organizes his own gang and leads a double life as a receiver and 'thief-taker', denouncing any of his followers who give him trouble, and being rewarded for his public-spiritedness.

Mansell Collection

Mansell Collection

AMELIA
✦1752✦

Gambling is just one of Captain Billy Booth's weaknesses (right), but he and his beautiful wife Amelia are still in love. Though innocent, Booth is sent to prison, where conditions are utterly squalid – except for people like the courtesan Miss Matthews. She takes Booth into her cell, and he succumbs – so that on his release he is blackmailed into visiting her. Booth becomes a hardened gambler. Then a young lord takes an interest in Amelia . . .

THE JOURNAL OF A VOYAGE TO LISBON
✦1755✦

In 1754 Fielding was carried aboard a ship bound for Portugal (below), hoping for a respite from his many crippling ailments. Despite the pain he must have been suffering, his account of the voyage is as lively and observant as anything in his fiction, though touched by poignancy. He called the book 'a novel without a plot' and, eschewing the traditional fabulous adventures and sea monsters associated with travel books of the time, described life aboard the *Queen of Portugal* and the eccentricities of her skipper, Captain Veal. The work is dappled by moments of despair, for the voyage entailed 'the most disagreeable hours which ever haunted the author'.

Gaspare Traversi: The Card Party/Musée des Beaux-Arts, Rouen/Giraudon/Bridgeman Art Library

Samuel Scott: Custom House Quay (detail)/Fishmongers' Hall, London/Bridgeman Art Library

Rough Justice

**Fielding was an unusually humane magistrate at a time
when other law enforcers tried to deter criminals by
meting out the harshest and most brutal punishments.**

Many novelists write about crime and the seamy side of life, but few can have had such close acquaintance with these subjects as Henry Fielding – Principal Justice of the Peace for Middlesex and Westminster. From the bench he saw all types of offender, from the hardened professional thug to the poor wretch driven to crime by desperation.

Fielding was one of the enlightened few who saw a connection between poverty and crime. "The sufferings of the Poor", he noted in his *Proposal for Making an effectual Provision for the Poor*, "are indeed less observed than their misdeeds; not from any want of compassion, but because they are less well known, and this is the true reason why we hear them so often mentioned with abhorrence, and so seldom with pity. They starve

and freeze and rot among themselves, but they beg and steal and rob among their betters."

Most of the administrators of the law were much more hard-hearted, however, and there are cases in Fielding's time of children as young as seven being hanged for what would now be considered petty theft. Such ruthlessness was possible because life in general was held very cheap.

Up to one in five babies died before their first year and only one in three infants reached the age of five. In the poorest of London boroughs in the 1740s three in every four children died before the age of six. Even the richest and most privileged were not immune – indeed none of Queen Anne's 17 children survived infancy.

Many people lived in appalling squalor, and few

Gin Lane
*(above) Hogarth's famous
engraving illustrates the
social evils that gin-
drinking created. His
hope in issuing it was 'to
reform some reigning
Vices peculiar to the lower
Class of People'.*

Danger on the road
*(left and far left) In the
18th century the roads
were plagued by
highwaymen, and – then
as now – crime made
good material for
sensational journalism.*

In rural England one in five of the population received Poor Law Relief. By an Act of Parliament of 1722 parishes were allowed to build workhouses, or what one contemporary called 'houses of terror', to accommodate them. Those who refused 'to be lodged, kept or maintained in such a house' would, according to the Act, forfeit their right to relief.

It was a corrupt system. Unpaid overseers, appointed by magistrates to run them, were motivated by profit rather than compassion. In some workhouses men, women and children were mixed in with the old, the sick and the insane (many of whom were held in chains). Of 2339 children admitted into London workhouses between the years 1750 and 1755, only 168 survived.

AN ORGY OF DRINKING

People sought stimulation, release and oblivion through drink. In an age when physical pain was everyone's lot and few medicines were available, alcohol was the only widely available painkiller. But even allowing for the fact that drink was cheap, the amount consumed was prodigious. Gin was drunk by the pint, and Fielding (writing in 1751) observed that it was 'the principal Sustenance (if it may be so called) of more than one

Nest of thieves
Criminals often operated in groups, and pickpockets in particular were noted for the slickness of their teamwork. Here members of the 'fairer sex' display their skills at robbing their victim.

Guardian of the peace
Nightwatchmen such as the one below were meant to make it difficult for criminals to operate at night, but they were generally too old, decrepit or cowardly to be a serious deterrent.

questioned the extremes of wealth and poverty that existed at the time. To the aristocracy and landed gentry, who formed only two per cent of the population but owned most of the nation's wealth, the poor were almost another species. The Duchess of Buckingham loathed Methodists because, she said, 'it is monstrous to be told that you have a heart as sinful as the common wretches that crawl on the earth. This is highly offensive and insulting and at variance with high rank and good breeding.'

The bulk of the population, 80 per cent, lived in the countryside. For them life was little better than for the London poor. Few of them ever ventured beyond their parish boundary. Those who did shared the roads with highwaymen and gibbeted corpses and their beds in country inns at night with strangers and fleas.

Reforming magistrate
Fielding's blind half-brother, Sir John Fielding, was zealous in stamping out professional crime and a pioneer in the humane treatment of juvenile offenders. His blindness sharpened his other senses; he could reputedly recognize hundreds of criminals by their voices.

Home from the sea
Dock areas were notoriously rough places, for sailors in port freely indulged in drinking, gambling and sex with prostitutes – which often led to violent crimes.

hundred thousand people in this Metropolis. Many of these Wretches there are, who swallow Pints of this Poison within the Twenty Four Hours; the dreadful Effects of which I have the Misfortune every Day to see, and to smell too.'

The orgy of gin-drinking was immortalized in Hogarth's engraving *Gin Lane* (1751). It is estimated that during the height of the 'gin craze' there were 6000 places in London (excluding the City and the south-west side of the Thames) where the drink was openly sold. In one of the largest parishes every fifth house retailed it. Gin could be bought from street stalls and barrows, chandlers, tobacconists, garrets and cellars.

The case of a nurse at a christening at Beddington in Surrey shows how drinking frequently led to tragedy. 'The nurse was so intoxicated', runs an article in *The Gentleman's Magazine* for 1748, 'that after undressing the child, instead of lying it in the cradle, she put it behind a large fire, which burnt it to death . . . She was examined before a magistrate, and said she was quite stupid and senseless, so that she took the child for a log of wood; on which she was discharged.'

HONOUR AMONG THIEVES

The lawlessness of London struck many foreign visitors. 'Pickpockets are legion' wrote the Frenchman César de Saussure. 'With extraordinary dexterity they steal handkerchiefs, snuff-boxes, watches – in short anything they can find in your pockets. Their profession is practised in the streets, in churches, at the play, and especially in crowds . . . These rascals are so impudent, they will steal even under the gibbet.'

His thoughts were echoed by *The London Magazine* of 1748, where it was noted that 'not only pickpockets, but street-robbers and highwaymen, are grown to such a pitch of insolence at this time, robbing in gangs, defying authority, and often rescuing their companions and carrying them off in triumph.'

The reference to rescue illustrates the idea of 'honour among thieves' and the romantic gloss that is often attached to the criminal underworld of the time. Highwaymen were the most glamorous figures of all, but in reality they were mainly ruthless thugs rather than the chivalrous rogues of popular legend.

In August 1750 Horace Walpole, the writer and art connoisseur, noted in his diary, 'a highwayman attacked a post-chaise in Piccadilly within fifty yards of this house; the fellow was pursued, rode over the watchman, almost killed him, and escaped.' Such incidents were common. *The General Advertiser* reported on 5 February 1750 'near forty highwaymen, street robbers, burglars, rogues, vagabonds and cheats have been committed within a week last past by Justice Fielding'.

In the dimly-lit streets, alleyways and lanes of London criminals could snatch a purse, waylay pedestrians or attack coaches unobserved. With no proper police force, offenders stood a good chance of escape. The adminstration of law and order was

generally chaotic and corrupt. Unpaid constables, of whom there were only 80 in the City of Westminster, received a reward of £40 for each highwayman, robber and housebreaker who was apprehended and convicted, but few took their duties seriously and most kept out of the way at the first whiff of trouble. Watchmen, mostly old and decrepit, were paid one shilling and sixpence a night for their services. Too feeble to apprehend anyone, most spent their hours of duty drinking.

The brothers Fielding were leaders in trying to rectify this situation. In 1749 they formed a small force of men known as the Bow Street Runners, who were forerunners of today's British police. They did their job well, but were too few in number to make more than a local impact.

PRISON CONDITIONS

Many offenders or suspected offenders were captured, however, by self-appointed thief-takers, vile criminals themselves who betrayed or even set up their fellows. Arrested, the offender was marched off to jail to await trial. This might be a common jail – the county jails of the provinces or big city jails or those run by private enterprise – or, because of the chronic over-crowding, a bridewell or house of correction. Bridewells existed all over the country and were small, often ruinous lock-ups housing vagrants and minor offenders as well as felons. Molly Seagrim is incarcerated in one in *Tom Jones*.

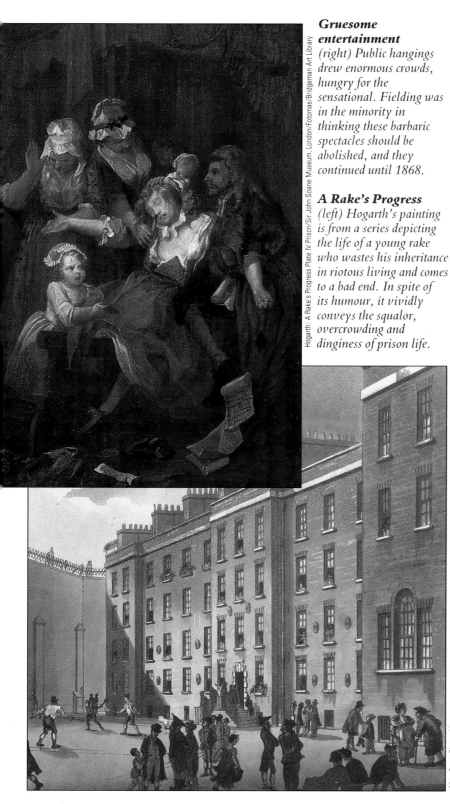

Gruesome entertainment

(right) Public hangings drew enormous crowds, hungry for the sensational. Fielding was in the minority in thinking these barbaric spectacles should be abolished, and they continued until 1868.

A Rake's Progress

(left) Hogarth's painting is from a series depicting the life of a young rake who wastes his inheritance in riotous living and comes to a bad end. In spite of its humour, it vividly conveys the squalor, overcrowding and dinginess of prison life.

there was no outdoor courtyard for them to take exercise, prisoners might spend all their time locked up. They slept in foul dungeons either strung to fellow-prisoners and chained to the floor or on stinking straw. Few prisons had adequate ventilation because there was a tax on windows.

Food, to which prisoners awaiting trial had no legal right, was meagre. Writing in 1773, when conditions were better than at mid-century, the prison-reformer John Howard noted that 'many criminals are half-starved; such of them as at their commitment were in health, come out famished, scarce able to move and for weeks incapable of labour'. Many prisoners died long before trial from 'jail fever' (typhus), 'putrid fevers' and small-pox. In one notorious case at the Old Bailey in May 1750, 100 disease-ridden prisoners from Newgate were tried in a hall 30ft square, packed with spectators. Of six judges on the bench four died, together with forty officials and jurors.

CRUEL PUNISHMENTS

The length of time that prisoners, innocent or guilty, rotted while awaiting trial varied from place to place. In some counties the assizes met only once a year; in Hull it was once every three years in the 1770s; before then it had been every seven years.

As the century progressed, the lack of an effective police force to halt the increasing crime rate led to a stiffening of the penal code. The theory was that one thief on the gallows would terrify other thieves into honest ways. There is little evidence to suggest that such a deterrent was effective. Penalties were grossly unequal. To steal fruit ready gathered was a felony, the penalty for which was hanging. To gather fruit and steal it counted only as trespass, for which the punishment might be whipping or fining or both. Convicted whores were stripped to the waist and whipped. Mother Needham, a brothel-keeper and subject of Hogarth's *A Harlot's Progress*, was viciously pelted in the pillory in May 1731 and subsequently died. Until 1789 women could still be burned alive at the stake for murdering their husbands. Generally,

In the common jail newly arrived prisoners were greeted by the cry 'pay or strip'. Under this system prisoners were required to pay 'garnish', or entrance fee, to their fellow-prisoners. The amount varied from prison to prison. At Horsham in Sussex it was 6s 6d, at Newgate 2s 6d. Those unable to pay were deprived of their clothes.

Prisoners were locked up from sunset until six or eight the following morning. Except in small jails, men were usually separated from women. If

Debtors' prison

The Fleet Prison was London's main debtors' prison. Life there could be tolerable, as this picture shows. But many debtors rotted away in prison, with no opportunity of making amends for their 'crime'.

Caught in the act
Poaching was one of the commonest crimes in the 18th century and offenders were often dealt with harshly – more like serious criminals than unfortunates trying to supplement a meagre diet.

Cruel sports
Cock-fighting (below right) was one of the bloodthirsty entertainments enjoyed by Fielding's contemporaries. The callous indifference to suffering extended to humans, too.

Bloody riots
There were many riots in England in the 18th century, but the worst were the anti-Catholic Gordon Riots of 1780, named after the Protestant fanatic Lord George Gordon. Over 800 people died.

punishment reflected the interests of the ruling class, the landowners. Poachers, for example, were the most zealously punished by magistrates. Sheep-stealing was punishable by death.

In 1718 transportation for seven years had been introduced as an alternative punishment to branding (in which the victim was branded in the brawn of the left hand) or whipping. Before the loss of the American colonies in 1776, those transported were sent to Maryland or Virginia; thereafter Australia became the destination.

In 1768 judges had been empowered to substitute transportation for life for the death sentence, but even before this, those condemned to death did not always go to the gallows. Although there

were over 200 different offences for which death could be the punishment, on average no more than 200 people altogether were hanged in England and Wales each year. Chances of a reprieve depended on where you lived. From 1752 to 1772 more than half of those sentenced to death in London went to the gallows, while in Norfolk it was less than a third, and in the Midlands less than a quarter.

MOB RULE

In London a hanging was a recognized holiday and public entertainment. As Fielding remarks in *Tom Jones*, "If our reader delights in seeing executions, I think he ought not to lose any time in taking a first row at Tyburn." Such was the popularity of hangings that at Tyburn (where Marble Arch now stands in Oxford Street) permanent wooden grandstands, known as Mother Proctor's pews, were erected. When Earl Ferrers was hanged for murder in 1760, Mother Proctor collected a handsome £500 in receipts. But a crowd deprived of their pleasure could turn nasty. In 1735, according to a report in *The Gentleman's Magazine*, a mob in Bristol, cheated of a hanging when the victim poisoned himself, dug up the suicide's body and 'dragged his guts about the highway, poked his eyes out and broke almost all his bones'.

Mobs frequently took the law into their own hands in this way. Rioting, indeed, seems almost to have become a way of life in eighteenth century England. The theatre at Drury Lane was wrecked by rioters six times during the century. Bread and food riots were endemic. In 1740 Norwich was paralysed for five days by rioters protesting about the price of mackerel. On 30 June 1749 two sailors were allegedly robbed at a bawdy house called 'The Crown' in London. Getting no satisfaction from the brothel-keeper, they returned with their shipmates and proceeded to wreck the place. Troops were called, but took until three in the morning to quell the riot.

FIELDING TO THE RESCUE

On the following evening 400 sailors returned, threatening to pull down all bawdy houses, and proceeded to destroy 'The Star'. Some days later their numbers had swollen to 3000. Fielding, as magistrate, acted promptly, appealing to the government for reinforcements. When peace was finally restored, only seven rioters had been arrested. Of these, two were found guilty under the Riot Act and one was eventually hanged.

Rioting was just one aspect of the violence that was accepted as a fact of life. Children were thrashed at home, flogged at school and brutalized at work. Homosexuals were stoned to death in the pillory. Blood sports, such as cock-fighting, drew large crowds. Smugglers had little compunction about murdering excise officers: caught smuggling they would be hanged anyway. To many contemporaries it seemed, as Henry Fielding was to write in the *Covent Garden Journal* in 1752, that Sodom and Gomorrah were only 'somewhat worse than we are now'.

BIBLIOGRAPHY

Ashley, Maurice, *Charles I and Cromwell.* Routledge, Chapman & Hall (New York, 1988)

Atkyns, Richard, and Gwyn, John, *The Civil War.* Shoe String Press (Hamden, 1967)

Barber, C. L., *Creating Elizabethan Tragedy: The Theatre of Marlow and Kyd.* University of Chicago Press (Chicago, 1988)

Barroll, J. Leeds, *Shakespearean Tragedy.* Folger Books (Cranbury, 1984)

Bindman, David, *Hogarth.* Thames & Hudson (New York, 1985)

Bradford, G., *Samuel Pepys.* Haskell Booksellers (Brooklyn, 1974)

Brittain, Vera, *Valiant Pilgrim: The Story of John Bunyan and Puritan England.* Richard West (Philadelphia, 1950)

Brown, Ivor, *Shakespeare in His Time* (reprint of 1960 edition). Century Bookbindery (Philadelphia, 1982)

Bruns, Roger, *Julius Caesar.* Chelsea House (New York, 1987)

Canfield, J. Douglas, *Nicholas Rowe and Christian Tragedy.* University Presses of Florida (Gainesville, 1977)

Cleary, Thomas, *Henry Fielding: Political Writer.* Humanities Press International (Atlantic Highlands, 1984)

De Voogd, Peter, *Henry Fielding and William Hogarth: The Correspondence of the Arts.* Humanities Press International (Atlantic Highlands, 1981)

Dircks, Richard J., *Henry Fielding.* G. K. Hall (Boston, 1983)

Dixon-Scott, James, *John Bunyan's England* (reprint of 1928 edition). Folcroft (Folcroft, 1977)

Dowden, Edward, *Introduction to Shakespeare.* Folcroft (Folcroft, 1973)

Downes, Kerry, *The Architecture of Wren.* Universe Books (New York, 1982)

Earle, Peter, *The Life and Times of Henry V.* Biblio Distribution Center (Totowa, 1972)

Ellis-Fermor, Una, *Shakespeare the Dramatist.* Folcroft (Folcroft, 1948)

Emden, Cecil S., *Pepys Himself* (reprint of 1963 edition). Greenwood Press (Westport, 1980)

Erickson, Carolly, *The First Elizabeth.* Summit Books (New York, 1984)

Furnivall, F. J., and Munro, John, *Shakespeare's Life and Work.* Folcroft (Folcroft, 1973)

Haynes, Alan, *The White Bear: Robert Dudley, the Elizabethan Earl of Leicester.* Dufour Editions (Chester Springs, 1987)

Heilman, Robert B., *Shakespeare; The Tragedies: Twentieth Century Views, New Perspectives.* Prentice Hall (Englewood Cliffs, 1984)

Hill, Christopher, *A Tinker and a Poor Man: John Bunyan and His Church, 1628-1688.* Alfred A. Knopf (New York, 1989)

Hume, Robert D., *Henry Fielding and the London Theatre, 1728-1737.* Oxford University Press (New York, 1988)

Hunt, Percival, *Samuel Pepys in the Diary* (reprint of 1958 edition). Greenwood Press (Westport, 1978)

Hutton, Ronald, *The Restoration: A Political and Religious History of England and Wales 1658-1667* Oxford University Press (New York, 1985)

Jones, J. R., *Charles II: Royal Politician.* Unwin Hyman (Winchester, 1987)

Lees-Milne, James, *The Age of Inigo Jones.* Somerset Publications (New York, 1953)

Morley, John M., *Walpole* (reprint of 1889 edition). Greenwood Press (Westport, 1971)

Pease, T. C., *The Leveller Movement.* Peter Smith (Magnolia, 1988)

Pinciss, Gerald M., *Christopher Marlowe.* Ungar Publishing (New York, 1975)

Ponsonby, Arthur, *John Evelyn.* Folcroft (Folcroft, 1933)

Sirianni, Frank A., *Antony and Cleopatra: The Reality Behind the Myth.* Vantage Press (New York, 1988)

Sorrell, Tom, *Hobbes.* Routledge, Chapman & Hall (New York, 1986)

Speight, Harold E., *The Life and Writings of John Bunyan.* Arden Library (Darby, 1983)

Tanner, J. R., *Samuel Pepys and the Royal Navy* (reprint of 1920 edition). Folcroft (Folcroft, 1974)

Varey, Simon, *Henry Fielding.* Cambridge University Press (New York, 1986)

Wheatley, P., *Samuel Pepys and the World He Lived In.* Haskell Booksellers (Brooklyn, 1977)

White, W. H., *John Bunyan* (reprint of 1895 edition). Arden Library (Darby, 1985)

INDEX